Crisis of Conscience

Crisis of Conscience

Edited by

John M. Haas

A Crossroad Herder Book
The Crossroad Publishing Company
New York

1996

The Crossroad Publishing Company
370 Lexington Avenue, New York, NY 10017

Printed in the United States of America

Library of Congress Cataloging-in-Publication Data

Crisis of conscience / edited by John Haas.
    p. cm.
    "A Crossroad Herder Book."
    Papers presented at a conference in Orvieto, Italy, May 27, 1994.
    Includes index.
    ISBN 0-8245-1577-3 (pbk.)
    1. Christian ethics–Catholic authors–Congresses.   2. Conscience–
Congresses.   3. Civilization, Modern–20th century–Congresses.
    4. Catholic Church–Doctrines–Congresses.   I. Haas, John (John M.).
BJ1249.C74   1996
241'.1–dc20
                                     96-5990
                                       CIP

Contents

Foreword: Crisis of Conscience vii
    JOHN M. HAAS

Letter from Joseph Cardinal Ratzinger xiii

1. Conscience and Truth 1
    JOSEPH CARDINAL RATZINGER

2. Crisis of Conscience and Culture 21
    JOHN M. HAAS

3. Conscience and the *Liberum Arbitrium* 51
    WOJCIECH GIERTYCH, O.P.

4. Conscience, Truth, and Prudence 79
    SERVAIS PINCKAERS, O.P.

5. Conscience and the Object of the Moral Act 93
    RALPH MCINERNY

6. Conscience and Responsibility in Christian Ethics 111
    ROBERT SPAEMANN

7. Pastoral Practice and Conscience 135
    IGNACIO CARRASCO DE PAULA

8. The Autonomy of Conscience and Subjection to Truth 149
    CARLO CAFFARRA

Index 169

Foreword

Crisis of Conscience

JOHN M. HAAS

Friday morning, May 27, 1994, the sun shone on the hilltop town of Orvieto rising above the broad Paglia Valley north of Rome. The appearance of Olympian tranquility atop the tufa plateau with the town's brilliant jewel of a Gothic cathedral with its unique stripes of alternating white and gray stone belied a tumultuous history going back to Etruscan times. The sheer cliffs dropping off at the edges of the plateau provided a natural fortification for the town, so that over the centuries protective walls never had to be built.

The Romans had flourished in the rich agricultural region in classical times, while Alaric and Odoacer had occupied the town during the barbarian invasions; the great Roman general Belisarius regained it from the Goths in 538. Possession of Orvieto passed through many hands over the centuries–from the inhabitants of the town when it was an independent city-state in the twelfth century to the French Pope Martin IV in the thirteenth century to the King of a united Italy in the nineteenth. It was seldom free of the strife that swept over Umbria century after century.

On that spring day in 1994 six Catholic moral philosophers and theologians had gathered in the eighth century Benedictine Abbey of Sts. Severo and Martirio in the Paglia Valley with Orvieto rising majestically in the distance. They were engaged in a raging intellectual and moral struggle, not a political or military one. They had gathered to discuss what all perceived to be a "crisis of conscience" in the Christian world, one that had resulted, according to Pope John Paul II in his encyclical *Veritatis Splendor*, from the increased inability in our day to distinguish between good and evil.

Shortly before these Catholic intellectuals gathered, three German bishops from the Upper Rhine province had created a stir of controversy in the church by establishing "principles of pastoral care" by which divorced and remarried Catholics could receive Holy Communion despite the fact of their living in what Catholic doctrine and discipline had always held to be an objective state of sin. Since the church, accepting the teachings of Christ on marriage, does not recognize divorce, those who presume to attempt marriage after receiving a civil divorce without an ecclesiastical annulment are viewed as being in an objectively adulterous relationship.

The policy of the three German bishops was met with incredulity by many in the church. And of course there were the customary appeals to conscience in their policy statement: "Through clarifying pastoral dialogue between the partners of a second marriage and a priest . . . it can happen in individual cases that the marriage partners (or else just one of the partners) see their (or his/her) conscience clear to approach the table of the Lord. . . . Such a decision can only be made by the individual in a personal review of his or her conscience and no one else." This unprecedented action seemed to be the latest, and most highly sanctioned, disorder to have resulted from almost three decades of novel moral theological opinion that appeared to void morality of its objective content and to make it a means of justifying subjective rationalizations for individual conduct. The policy was later declared to be untenable by the Congregation for the Doctrine of the Faith.[1]

Msgr. Eugene V. Clark, Ph.D., President of the Wethersfield Institute of New York, conceived of the idea of a conference to discuss the particular problem of the crisis of conscience that he was convinced lay at the heart of our contemporary moral confusion. The Wethersfield Institute enlisted my assistance in organizing the conference. Working with Msgr. Clark and Patricia Donahoe, Program Director at The Wethersfield Institute, the decision was made to make the conference international and to enlist a small number of the leading Catholic moralists in the Christian world to address the deep crisis in morality in our day by concentrating on the question of conscience.

His Eminence, Joseph Cardinal Ratzinger, Prefect of the Congregation for the Doctrine of the Faith, accepted our invitation to attend the conference and gave us permission to use an address, "Conscience and Truth," which he had delivered in February 1991 to the United States bishops gathered at a moral theology workshop in Dallas, Texas, as a point of reference for our discussions in Orvieto. Other documents to which we were keenly sensitive were the section on conscience in *Gaudium et Spes* (no. 16) and the encyclical *Veritatis Splendor*, which had just been issued by John Paul II.

All those whom we invited to present papers at the conference graciously accepted. Their papers, along with Cardinal Ratzinger's address to the American bishops and an opening chapter by me, comprise the chapters of this book.

Dr. Robert Spaemann is professor of philosophy at the University of Munich and has published, among many other titles, *Moralische Grundbegriffe und Glück und Wohlwollen: Versuch Über Ethik.* Dr. Ralph McInerny is the Michael P. Grace Professor of Medieval Studies at the University of Notre Dame and Director of the Jacques Maritain Center. Also widely published, Professor McInerny has written *Ethica Thomistica, The Question of Christian Ethics,* and *Moral Action in Aquinas.* The Reverend Dr. Servais Pinckaers, O.P., is professor of moral theology at the University of Fribourg in Switzerland and author of *Les Actes Humains, Le Renouveau de la Morale, La Morale Catholique, L'Evangile et la Morale,* and *The Sources of Christian Ethics.*

The Reverend Professor Carlo Caffarra, President of the *Instituto Giovanni Paolo II per Studi Du Matrimonio e Famiglia* at the Lateran University in Rome at the time of the conference, has since been ordained a bishop and appointed Archbishop of Ferrarra-Comacchio in Italy. He has several books in Italian, is the director of and contributor to the international journal *Anthropotes,* and has a book in English entitled *Living in Christ: Fundamental Principles of Catholic Moral Teaching.* The Reverend Professor Ignacio Carrasco de Paula is a Spanish physician and priest of the Prelature of Opus Dei. Msgr. Carrasco was formerly Rector of the *Ateneo Romano della Santa Croce* in Rome, where he is now a faculty member. He is also a member of the Pontifical

Council for Assistance to Health Care Workers. The Reverend Dr. Wojciech Giertych, O.P., is a professor of moral theology at the Dominican House of Studies in Cracow, Poland; he lived and taught for a number of years in England.

Also in attendance at the conference as observers and commentators on the papers were the Reverend Graziano Borgonovo of the University of Fribourg; the Reverend Father Romanus Cessario, O.P., of the Dominican House of Studies in Washington, D.C.; the Reverend Dr. Modesto Santos, professor of ethics and Vice Dean of the Ecclesiastical Faculty of Philosophy at the University of Navarra in Pamplona, Spain; the Reverend Fathers Charles Brown, Gerald Murray, Donald Haggerty, and Christopher Hartley, all priests of the Archdiocese of New York who were engaged in graduate studies in Rome; the Jesuit Fathers Peter Ryan and Paul Shaunessy; the Reverend Father Robert Gahl of the *Ateneo Romano*; and the Reverend Father Stanislaw Warzeszak of Warsaw.

Cardinal Ratzinger had to cancel his participation in the conference at the last moment, because the English translation of *The Catechism of the Catholic Church* was being presented to the Holy Father at the same time as our meeting. Regrettably, Msgr. Clark of The Homeland Foundation was also unable to attend. Patricia Donahoe of The Wethersfield Institute with her organizing genius was present, as well as Mary Ann Nobile of Paris, whose Nobile Language Services provided excellent translations of all the papers. The participants were able to provide perspectives on the problem of conscience from their own cultural and linguistic groups, which included English, Polish, Italian, Spanish, French, and German.

The refined sense of history and the exquisite good taste of Msgr. Clark had led us to the ancient Abbey of Sts. Severo and Martirio, known today as the La Badia, which has been magnificently restored as a beautiful hotel by the Umbrian Counts Fiumi di Sterpeto. La Badia itself, combining Romanesque and Lombardesque elements with the Gothic style of the Prémontré Canons who later occupied the monastery, provided a sense of the long and tortuous history of Europe under the civilizing effects of the Catholic faith. A twelve-sided tower at the monastery, reminiscent of the twelve apostles and commissioned by the Countess Matilde di Canossa in the twelfth century, kept watch over our proceedings. Mass was celebrated daily in the ancient Church of the Crucifixion with its twelfth-century high altar supported by two Roman bas-reliefs. Normally closed, the church was opened specially for our use during the conference.

Msgr. Clark, even in his absence, had graciously made arrangements for the participants to be entertained by the *Associazione Corale Una Voce* of Rome, which often sings in the Sistine Chapel. In the former refectory of the abbey, surrounded by frescoes of the twelfth to fourteenth centuries, the participants enjoyed a concert of "Pilgrimages, Feasts, and Celebrations–Chants of Medieval Europe" under the direction of Maestro Carmelo G. Picone.

I know I speak for all those who were privileged to participate in the unique Orvieto conference on conscience in expressing our deepest gratitude to Msgr. Eugene Clark of The Wethersfield Institute, ably assisted by Patricia Donahoe, for the gracious kindnesses extended to us and especially for their obvious deep commitment to Catholic truth and Catholic culture.

I would also like to express my particular gratitude to Mary Ann Nobile and Beth Ann Siro for their assistance in preparing the manuscripts for publication.

Note

1. On September 14, 1994, the Congregation for the Doctrine of the Faith published the opinion that the "pastoral principles" of the Rhineland bishops were untenable. It stated: "The mistaken conviction of a divorced-and-remarried person that he may receive Holy Communion normally presupposes that personal conscience is considered in the final analysis to be able, on the basis of one's own convictions, to come to a decision about the existence or absence of a previous marriage and the value of the new union. However, such a position is inadmissible. . . . The judgment of conscience of one's own marital situation does not regard only the immediate relationship between man and God, as if one could prescind from the church's mediation that also includes canonical laws binding in conscience. Not to recognize this essential aspect would mean in fact to deny that marriage is a reality of the church, that is to say, a sacrament." For those wanting to gain greater knowledge of this issue, see *Origins*, 10 March 1994, and *Origins*, 27 October 1994.

Letter from Joseph Cardinal Ratzinger

Vatican City
23.IV.1994

Reverend Fathers and Esteemed Gentlemen:

Please accept my sincere words of encouragement for your efforts at the Orvieto Conference on Conscience sponsored by The Wethersfield Institute. It is a joy to know that men of such learning and deep faith have directed their erudition to this most critical topic.

Although we must always be bound by conscience, some of the greatest crimes of our own day have been committed, and are being committed, by an appeal to individual conscience, as though there were no higher norm. But as our Holy Father said in *Veritatis Splendor*: "It is always from the *truth* that the dignity of conscience derives." Consequently, the act of conscience is not arbitrary. Conscience does not make the truth but only discerns and applies it. As St. Bonaventure teaches, "Conscience is like God's herald and messenger; it does not command things on its own authority, but commands them as coming from God's authority, like a herald when he proclaims the edict of the king." As we know, true conscience enables us to see what actions are actually for our good and the promotion of human happiness. I pray that your deliberations will help lead many to the peace and joy that can come only from a life lived in conformity with a true, well-formed conscience.

I truly regret that I will be unable to join you at the Orvieto Conference as I had hoped. However, I am very much encouraged knowing that you are addressing this critical subject with sound scholarship and fervent prayer. May our Lord richly bless your efforts.

With prayerful best wishes, I am
Sincerely in Christ,
Joseph Cardinal Ratzinger

Crisis of Conscience

1

Conscience and Truth

Joseph Cardinal Ratzinger

In the contemporary discussion on what constitutes the essence of
morality and how it can be recognized, the question of conscience has
become paramount, especially in the field of Catholic Moral Theology. This discussion centers on the concepts of freedom and norm,
autonomy and heteronomy, self-determination and external determination by authority. Conscience appears here as the bulwark of freedom in contrast to encroachments of authority on existence. In the
course of this, two notions of the Catholic are set in opposition to
each other. One is a renewed understanding of the Catholic essence
which expounds Christian faith from the basis of freedom and as the
very principle of freedom itself. The other is a superseded, "pre-con-
ciliar" model, which subjects Christian existence to authority, regulat-
ing life even into its most intimate preserves, and thereby attempts to
maintain control over people's lives. Morality of conscience and morality of authority, as two opposing models, appear to be locked in
struggle with each other. Accordingly, the freedom of the Christian

Originally published in *Catholic Conscience Foundation and Formation: Proceedings of the Tenth Bishops' Workshop*, ed., Russell E. Smith (Braintree, Mass.: Pope
John XXIII Medical-Moral Research and Education Center, 1991).

would be rescued by appeal to the classical principle of moral tradition that conscience is the highest norm which man is to follow even in opposition to authority. Authority, in this case, the Magisterium, may well speak of matters moral, but only in the sense of presenting conscience with material for its own deliberation. Conscience would retain, however, the final word. Some authors reduce conscience in this its aspect of final arbiter to the formula: conscience is infallible.[1]

Nonetheless, at this point, a contradiction can arise. It is of course undisputed that one must follow a certain conscience, or at least not act against it. But whether the judgment of conscience, or what one takes to be such, is always right, indeed whether it is infallible, is another question. For if this were the case, it would mean that there is no truth—at least not in moral and religious matters, which is to say, in the areas which constitute the very pillars of our existence. For judgments of conscience can contradict each other. Thus there could be at best the subject's own truth, which would be reduced to the subject's sincerity. No door or window would lead from the subject into the broader world of being and human solidarity. Whoever thinks this through will come to the realization that no real freedom exists then and that the supposed pronouncements of conscience are but the reflection of social circumstances. This should necessarily lead to the conclusion that placing freedom in opposition to authority overlooks something. There must be something deeper, if freedom and, therefore, human existence are to have meaning.

1. A Conversation on the Erroneous Conscience and First Inferences

It has become apparent that the question of conscience leads in fact to the core of the moral problem and thus to the question of man's existence itself. I would now like to pursue this question, not in the form of a strictly conceptual and therefore unavoidably abstract presentation, but by way of narrative, as one might say today, by relating, to begin with, the story of my own encounter with this problem. I first became aware of the question with all its urgency in the beginning of my academic teaching. In the course of a dispute, a senior colleague, who was keenly aware of the plight of being Christian in our times, expressed the opinion that one should actually be grateful to God that He allows there to be so many unbelievers in good conscience. For if their eyes were to be opened and they became believers, they would not be capable, in this world of ours, of bearing the burden of faith with all its moral obligations. But as it is, since they can go another way in good conscience they can still reach salvation. What shocked me about this assertion was not in the first place the idea of an erroneous conscience given by God Himself in order to save men by means of such artfulness–the idea, so to speak of a blindness sent by God for the salvation of those in question. What disturbed me was the notion it harbored that faith is a burden which can hardly be borne and which no doubt was intended only for stronger natures–faith almost as a kind of punishment, in any case, an imposition not easily coped with. According to this view, faith would not make salvation easier but harder. Being happy would mean not being burdened with having to believe or having to submit to the moral yoke of the faith of the Catholic Church. The erroneous conscience which makes life easier and marks a more human course, would then be the real grace, the normal way to salvation. Untruth, keeping truth at bay, would be better for man than truth. It would not be the truth that would set him free, but rather he would have to be freed from the truth. Man would be more at home in the dark than in the light. Faith would not be the good gift of the good God but instead an affliction. If this were the state of affairs, how could faith give rise to joy? Who would have the courage to pass faith on to others? Would it not be better to spare them the truth or even keep them from it? In the last few decades, notions of this sort have discernably crippled the disposition to evangelize. The one who sees the faith as a heavy burden or as a moral imposition is unable to invite others to believe. Rather he lets them be, in the putative freedom of their good consciences.

The one who spoke in this matter was a sincere believer, and, I would say, a strict Catholic who performed his moral duty with care and conviction. But he expressed a form of experience of faith which is disquieting. Its propagation could only be fatal to the faith. The almost traumatic aversion many have to what they hold to be "preconciliar" Catholicism is rooted, I am convinced, in the encounter with such a faith seen only as encumbrance. In this regard, to be sure, some very basic questions arise. Can such a faith actually be an encounter with truth? Is the truth about God and man so sad and difficult, or does truth not lie in the overcoming of such legalism? Does it not lie in freedom? But where does freedom lead? What course does it chart for us? At the conclusion, we shall come back to these fundamental problems of Christian existence today, but before we do that, we must return to the core of our topic, namely, the matter of conscience. As I said, what unsettled me in the argument just recounted was first of all the caricature of faith I perceived in it. In a second course of reflection, it occurred to me further that the concept of conscience which it implied must also be wrong. The erroneous conscience, by sheltering the person from the exacting demands of truth, saves him—thus went the argument. Conscience appeared here not as a window through which one can see outward to that common truth which founds and sustains us all, and so makes possible through the common recognition of truth the community of wants and responsibilities. Conscience here does not mean man's openness to the ground of his being, the power of perception for what is highest and most essential. Rather it appears as subjectivity's protective shell into which man can escape and there hide from reality. Liberalism's idea of conscience was in fact presupposed here. Conscience does not open the way to the redemptive road to truth which either does not exist or, if it does, is too demanding. It is the faculty which dispenses with truth. It thereby becomes the justification for subjectivity, which would like to have itself called into question. Similarly, it becomes the justification for social conformity. As mediating value between the different subjectivities, social conformity is intended to make living together possible. The obligation to seek the truth terminates, as do any doubts about the general inclination of society and what it has become accustomed to. Being convinced of oneself, as well as conforming to others, are sufficient. Man is reduced to his superficial conviction, and the less depth he has, the better for him.

What I was only dimly aware of in this conversation became glaringly clear a little later in a dispute among colleagues about the justifying power of the erroneous conscience. Objecting to this thesis, someone countered that if this were so then the SS people would be justified and we should seek them in heaven since they carried out all their atrocities with fanatic conviction and complete certainty of conscience. Another responded with utmost assurance that of course this was indeed the case. There is no doubting the fact that Hitler and his accomplices, who were deeply convinced of their cause, could not have acted otherwise. Therefore, the objective terribleness of their deeds notwithstanding, they acted morally, subjectively speaking. Since they followed their albeit mistaken consciences, one would have to recognize their conduct as moral and, as a result, should not doubt their eternal salvation. Since that conversation I knew with complete certainty that something was wrong with the theory of the justifying power of the subjective conscience, that, in other words, a concept of conscience which leads to such results must be false. Firm, subjective conviction and the lack of doubts and scruples which follow therefrom do not justify man. Some thirty years later, in the terse words of psychologist Albert Görres, I found summarized the perceptions I was trying to articulate. The elaboration of his insights forms the heart of this address. Görres shows that the feeling of guilt, the capacity to recognize guilt, belongs essentially to the spiritual make-up of man. This feeling of guilt disturbs the false calm of conscience and could be called conscience's complaint against my self-satisfied existence. It is as necessary for man as the physical pain which signifies disturbances of normal bodily functioning. Whoever is no longer capable of perceiving guilt is spiritually ill, "a living corpse, a dramatic character's mask," as Görres says.[2] "Monsters, among other brutes, are the ones without guilt feelings. Perhaps Hitler did not have any, or Himmler, or Stalin. Maybe Mafia bosses do not have any guilt feelings either, or maybe their remains are just well hidden in the cellar. Even aborted guilt feelings. . . . All men need guilt feelings."[3]

By the way, a look into Sacred Scripture should have precluded such diagnoses and such a theory of justification by the errant conscience. In Psalm 19:12-13, we find the ever worth pondering passage: "But who can discern his errors? Clear thou me from my unknown faults." That is not Old Testament objectivism, but profoundest human wisdom. No longer seeing one's guilt, the falling silent of conscience in so many areas, is an even more dangerous sickness of the soul than the guilt which one still recognizes as such. He who no longer notices that killing is a sin has fallen further than the one who still recognizes the shamefulness of his actions, because the former is further removed from the truth and conversion. Not without reason does the self-righteous man in the encounter with Jesus appear as the one who is really lost. If the tax collector with all his undisputed sins stands more justified before God than the pharisee with all his undeniably good works (Luke 18:9-14), this is not because the sins of the tax collector were not sins or the good deeds of the pharisee, not good deeds. Nor does it mean that the good that man does is not good before God, or the evil, not evil or at least not particularly important. The reason for this paradoxical judgment of God is shown precisely from our question. The pharisee no longer knows that he too has guilt. He has a completely clear conscience. But this silence of conscience makes him impenetrable to God and men, while the cry of conscience which plagues the tax collector makes him capable of truth and love. Jesus can move sinners. Not hiding behind the screen of their erroneous consciences, they have not become unreachable for the change which God expects of them—of us. He is ineffective with the "righteous," because they are not aware of any need for forgiveness and conversion. Their consciences no longer accuse them but justify them.

We find something similar in St. Paul, who tells us that the pagans, even without the law, knew quite well what God expected of them (Romans 2:1-16). The whole theory of salvation through ignorance breaks apart with this verse: There is present in man the truth, that is not to be repulsed, that one truth of the creator which in the revelation of salvation history has also been put in writing. Man can see the truth of God from the fact of his creaturehood. Not to see it is guilt. It is not seen because man does not want to see it. The "no" of the will which hinders recognition is guilt. The fact that the signal lamp does not shine is the consequence of a deliberate looking away from that which we do not wish to see.[4]

At this point of our reflections, it is possible to draw some initial conclusions with a view toward answering the question regarding the essence of conscience. We can now say: it will not do to identify man's conscience with the self-consciousness of the I, with its subjective certainty about itself and its moral behavior. On the one hand, this consciousness may be a mere reflection of the social surroundings and the opinions in circulation. On the other hand, it might also derive from a lack of self-criticism, a deficiency in listening to the depths of one's own soul. This diagnosis is confirmed by what has come to light since the fall of Marxist systems in Eastern Europe. The noblest and keenest minds of the liberated peoples speak of an enormous spiritual devastation which appeared in the years of the intellectual deformation. They speak of a blunting of the moral sense which is a more significant loss and danger than the economic damage that was done. The new patriarch of Moscow stressed this poignantly in the summer of 1990. The power of perception of people who lived in a system of deception was darkened. The society lost the capacity for mercy, and human feelings were forsaken. A whole generation was lost for the good, lost for human deeds. "We must lead society back to the eternal moral values," that is to say, open ears almost gone deaf, so that once again the promptings of God might be heard in human hearts. Error, the "erring" conscience, is only at first convenient. But then the silencing of conscience leads to the dehumanization of the world and to moral danger, if one does not work against it.

To put it differently, the identification of conscience with superficial consciousness, the reduction of man to his subjectivity, does not liberate but enslaves. It makes us totally dependent on the prevailing opinions and debases these with every passing day. Whoever equates conscience with superficial conviction, identifies conscience with a pseudo-rational certainty, a certainty which in fact has been woven from self-righteousness, conformity, and lethargy. Conscience is degraded to a mechanism for rationalization, while it should represent the transparency of the subject for the divine and thus constitute the very dignity and greatness of man. Conscience's reduction to subjective certitude betokens at the same time a retreat from truth. When the psalmist in anticipation of Jesus' view of sin and justice pleads for liberation from unconscious guilt, he points to the following relation. Certainly, one must follow an erroneous conscience. But the departure from truth which took place beforehand and now takes its revenge is the actual guilt which first lulls man into false security and then abandons him in the trackless waste.

2. *Newman and Socrates: Guides to Conscience*

At this juncture, I would like to make a temporary digression. Before we attempt to formulate reasonable answers to the questions regarding the essence of conscience, we must first widen the basis of our considerations somewhat, going beyond the personal which has thus far constituted our point of departure. To be sure, my purpose is not to try to develop a scholarly study on the history of theories of conscience, a subject on which different contributions have appeared just recently in fact.[5] I would prefer rather to stay with our approach thus far of example and narrative. A first glance should be directed to Cardinal Newman, whose life and work could be designated a single great commentary on the question of conscience. Nor should Newman be treated in a technical way. The given framework does not permit us to weigh the particulars of Newman's concept of conscience. I would simply like to try to indicate the place of conscience in the whole of Newman's life and thought. The insights gained from this will hopefully sharpen our view of present problems and establish the link to history, that is, both to the great witnesses of conscience and to the origin of the Christian doctrine of living according to conscience. When the subject of Newman and conscience is raised, the famous sentence from his letter to the Duke of Norfolk immediately comes to mind: "Certainly, if I am obliged to bring religion into after-dinner toasts, (which indeed does not seem quite the thing), I shall drink–to the Pope, if you please–still, to conscience first, and to the Pope afterwards."[6] In contrast to the statements of Gladstone, Newman sought to make a clear avowal of the papacy. And in contrast to mistaken forms of ultramontanism, Newman embraced an interpretation of the papacy, which is only then correctly conceived when it is viewed together with the primacy of conscience–a papacy not put in opposition to the primacy of conscience but based on it and guaranteeing it. Modern man, who presupposes the opposition of authority to subjectivity, has difficulty understanding this. For him, conscience stands on the side of subjectivity and is the expression of the freedom of the subject. Authority, on the other hand, appears to him as the constraint on, threat to, and even negation of freedom. So then we must go deeper to recover a vision in which this kind of opposition does not obtain.

For Newman the middle term which establishes the connection between authority and subjectivity is truth. I do not hesitate to say that truth is the central thought of Newman's intellectual grappling. Conscience is central for him because truth stands in the middle. To put it differently, the centrality of the concept conscience for Newman is linked to the prior centrality of the concept truth and can only be understood from this vantage point. The dominance of the idea of conscience in Newman does not signify that he, in the nineteenth century, and in contrast to "objectivistic" neoscholasticism, espoused a philosophy or theology of subjectivity. Certainly, the subject finds in Newman an attention which it had not received in Catholic theology perhaps since St. Augustine. But it is an attention in the line of Augustine and not in that of the subjectivist philosophy of the modern age. On the occasion of his elevation to Cardinal, Newman declared that most of his life was a struggle against the spirit of liberalism in religion; we might add, also against Christian subjectivism, as he found it in the evangelical movement of his time and which admittedly had provided him the first step on his lifelong road to conversion.[7] Conscience for Newman does not mean that the subject is the standard vis-à-vis the claims of authority in a truthless world, a world which lives from the compromise between the claims of the subject and the claims of the social order. Much more than that, conscience signifies the perceptible and demanding presence of the voice of truth in the subject himself. It is the overcoming of mere subjectivity in the encounter of the interiority of man with the truth from God. The verse Newman composed in 1833 in Sicily is characteristic: "I loved to choose and see my path; but now Lead thou me on!"[8] Newman's conversion to Catholicism was not for him a matter of personal taste or of subjective, spiritual need. He expressed himself on this even in 1844, on the threshold, so to speak, of his conversion: "No one can have a more unfavorable view than I of the present state of the Roman Catholics."[9] Newman was much more taken by the necessity to obey recognized truth than his own preferences, that is to say, even against his own sensitivity and bonds of friendship and ties due to similar backgrounds. It seems to me characteristic of Newman that he emphasized truth's priority over goodness in the order of virtues. Or, to put it in a way which is more understandable for us, he emphasized truth's priority over consensus, over the accommodation of groups. I would say, when we are speaking of a man of conscience, we mean one who looks at things this way. A man of conscience is one who never acquires tolerance, well-being, success, public standing, and approval on the part of prevailing opinion at the expense of truth. In this regard Newman is related to Britain's other great witness of conscience, Thomas More, for whom conscience was not at all an expression of subjective stubbornness or obstinate heroism. He numbered himself, in fact, among those fainthearted martyrs who only after faltering and much questioning succeed in mustering up obedience to conscience, mustering up obedience to the truth which must stand higher than any human tribunal or any type of personal taste.[10] Thus two standards become apparent for ascertaining the presence of a real voice of conscience. First, conscience is not identical to personal wishes and taste. Secondly, conscience cannot be reduced to social advantage, to group consensus, or to the demands of political and social power.

Let us take a side look now at the situation of our day. The individual may not achieve his advancement or well-being at the cost of betraying what he recognizes to be true; nor may humanity. Here we come in contact with the really critical issue of the modern age. The concept of truth has been virtually given up and replaced by the concept of progress. Progress itself "is" the truth. But through this seeming exaltation, progress loses its direction and becomes nullified. For if no direction exists, everything can just as well be regress as progress. Einstein's relativity theory properly concerns the physical cosmos. But it seems to me to describe exactly the situation of the intellectual/ spiritual world of our time. Relativity theory states there are no fixed systems of reference in the universe. When we declare a system to be a reference point from which we try to measure the whole, it is we who do the determining. Only in such a way can we attain any results at all. But the determination could always have been done differently. What we said about the physical cosmos is reflected in the second "Copernican revolution" regarding our basic relationship to reality. The truth as such, the absolute, the very reference point of thinking, is no longer visible. For this reason, precisely in the spiritual sense, there is no longer "up or down." There are no directions in a world without fixed measuring points. What we view to be direction is not based on a standard which is true in itself, but on our decision, and finally on considerations of expediency. In such a "relativistic" context, so-called teleological or consequentalist ethics ultimately becomes nihilistic, even if it fails to see this. And what is called conscience in such a worldview is, on deeper reflection, but a euphemistic way of saying that there is no such thing as an actual conscience, conscience understood as a "co-knowing" with the truth. Each person determines his own standards. And needless to say, in general relativity, no one can be of much help to the other, much less prescribe behavior to him.

At this point, the whole radicality of today's dispute over ethics and conscience, its center, becomes plain. It seems to me that the parallel in the history of thought is the quarrel between Socrates-Plato and the sophists in which the fateful decision between two fundamental positions has been rehearsed. There is on the one hand, the position of confidence in man's capacity for truth. On the other, there is a worldview in which man alone sets the standards for himself.[11] The fact that Socrates, the pagan, could become in a certain respect the prophet of Jesus Christ has its roots in this fundamental question. Socrates' taking up of this question bestowed on the way of philosophizing inspired by him a kind of salvation-historical privilege and made it an appropriate vessel for the Christian Logos. For with the Christian Logos we are dealing with liberation through truth and to truth. If you isolate Socrates' dispute from the accidents of the time and take into account his use of other arguments and terminology, you begin to see how much his is the same dilemma we face today. Giving up the idea of man's capacity for truth leads first to pure formalism in the use of words and concepts. Again, the loss of content, then and now, leads to a pure formalism of judgment. In many places today, for example, no one bothers any longer to ask what a person thinks. The verdict on someone's thinking is ready at hand as long as you can assign it to its corresponding, formal category: conservative, reactionary, fundamentalist, progressive, revolutionary. Assignment to a formal scheme suffices to render unnecessary coming to terms with the content. The same thing can be seen in more concentrated form in art. What a work of art says is indifferent. It can glorify God or the devil. The sole standard is that of formal, technical mastery.

We have now arrived at the heart of the matter. Where contents no longer count, where pure praxeology takes over, technique becomes the highest criterion. This means though, that power becomes the preeminent category, whether revolutionary or reactionary. This is precisely the distorted form of being like God of which the account of the fall speaks. The way of mere technical skill, the way of sheer power, is imitation of an idol and not expression of one's being made in the image and likeness of God. What characterizes man as man is not that he asks about the "can" but about the "should" and that he opens himself to the voice and demands of truth. It seems to me, this was the final meaning of the Socratic search, and it is the profoundest element in the witness of all martyrs. They attest to the fact that man's capacity for truth is a limit on all power and a guarantee of man's likeness to God. It is precisely in this way that the martyrs are the great witnesses of conscience, of that capability given to man to perceive the "should" beyond the "can" and thereby render possible real progress, real ascent.

3.   Systematic Consequences: The Two Levels of Conscience

a) Anamnesis

After all these ramblings through intellectual history, it is finally time to arrive at some conclusions, that is, to formulate a concept of conscience. The medieval tradition was right, I believe, in according two levels to the concept of conscience. These levels, though they can be well distinguished, must be continually referred to each other.[12] It seems to me, many unacceptable theses regarding conscience are the result of neglecting either the difference or the connection between the two. Mainstream scholasticism expressed these two levels in the concepts *synderesis* and *conscientia*. The word *synderesis* (*synteresis*) came into the medieval tradition of conscience from the stoic doctrine of the microcosm.[13] It remained unclear in its exact meaning and for this reason became a hindrance to a careful development of this essential aspect of the whole question of conscience. I would like, therefore, without entering into philosophical disputes, to replace this problematic word with the much more clearly defined Platonic concept of *anamnesis*. It is not only linguistically clearer and philosophically deeper and purer, but *anamnesis* above all also harmonizes with key motifs of biblical thought and the anthropology derived therefrom. The word *anamnesis* should be taken to mean exactly that which Paul expressed in the second chapter of his Letter to the Romans: "When Gentiles who have not the law do by nature what the law requires, they are a law to themselves, even though they do not have the law. They show that what the law requires is written on their hearts, while their conscience also bears witness (2:14f.)." The same thought is strikingly amplified in the great monastic rule of St. Basil. Here we read: "The love of God is not founded on a discipline imposed on us from outside, but is constitutively established in us as the capacity and necessity of our rational nature." Basil speaks in terms of "the spark of divine love which has been hidden in us," an expression which was to become important in medieval mysticism.[14] In the spirit of Johannine theology Basil knows that love consists in keeping the commandments. For this reason, the spark of love, which has been put into us by the creator, means this: "We have received interiorly beforehand the capacity and disposition for observing all divine commandments. . . . These are not something imposed from without." Referring everything back to its simple core, Augustine adds: "We could never judge that one thing is better than another, if a basic understanding of the good had not already been instilled in us."[15]

This means that the first so-called ontological level of the phenomenon conscience consists in the fact that something like an original memory of the good and true (both are identical) has been implanted in us, that there is an inner ontological tendency within man, who is created in the likeness of God, toward the divine. From its origin, man's being resonates with some things and clashes with others. This *anamnesis* of the origin, which results from the godlike constitution of our being is not a conceptually articulated knowing, a store of retrievable contents. It is so to speak an inner sense, a capacity to recall, so that the one whom it addresses, if he is not turned in on himself, hears its echo from within. He sees: That's it! That is what my nature points to and seeks.

The possibility for and right to mission rest on this *anamnesis* of the Creator which is identical to the ground of our existence. The gospel may, indeed, must be proclaimed to the pagans because they themselves are yearning for it in the hidden recesses of their souls (cf. Isaiah 42:4). Mission is vindicated then when those addressed recognize in the encounter with the word of the gospel that this indeed is what they have been waiting for. In this sense, Paul can say: the gentiles are a law to themselves—not in the sense of the modern liberal notions of autonomy which preclude transcendence of the subject, but in the much deeper sense that nothing belongs less to me than I myself. My own I is the site of the profoundest surpassing of self and contact with him from whom I came and toward whom I am going. In these sentences, Paul expresses the experience which he had as missionary to the gentiles and which Israel may have experienced before him in dealings with the "god-fearing." Israel could have experienced among the gentiles what the ambassadors of Jesus Christ found reconfirmed. Their proclamation answered an expectation. Their proclamation encountered an antecedent basic knowledge of the essential constants of the will of God which came to be written down in the commandments, which can be found in all cultures, and which can be all the more clearly elucidated the less an overbearing cultural bias distorts this primordial knowledge The more man lives in "fear of the Lord"– consider the story of Cornelius (especially, Acts 10:34-35)–the more concretely and clearly effective this *anamnesis* becomes.

Again let us take a formulation of St. Basil. The love of God, which is concrete in the commandments, is not imposed on us from without, the Church Father emphasizes, but has been implanted in us beforehand. The sense of the good has been stamped upon us, Augustine puts it. We can now appreciate Newman's toast first to conscience and then to the pope. The pope cannot impose commandments on faithful Catholics because he wants to or finds it expedient. Such a modern, voluntaristic concept of authority can only distort the true theological meaning of the papacy. The true nature of the Petrine office has become so incomprehensible in the modern age no doubt because we only think of authority in terms which do not allow for bridges between subject and object. Accordingly, everything which does not come from the subject is thought to be externally imposed. But the situation is really quite different according to the anthropology of conscience which we have tried to come to an appreciation of in these reflections. The *anamnesis* instilled in our being needs, one might say, assistance from without so that it can become aware of itself. But this "from without" is not something set in opposition to *anamnesis* but ordered to it. It has a maieutic function, imposes nothing foreign, but brings to fruition what is proper to *anamnesis,* namely, its interior openness to the truth. When we are dealing with the question of faith and church whose radius extends from the redeeming Logos over the gift of creation, we must, however, take into account yet another dimension which is especially developed in the Johannine writings. John is familiar with the *anamnesis* of the new "we" which is granted to us in the incorporation into Christ (one body, that is, one I with him). In remembering they knew him, the gospel has it in a number of places. The original encounter with Jesus gave the disciples what all generations thereafter receive in their foundational encounter with the Lord in Baptism and the Eucharist, namely, the new *anamnesis* of faith which unfolds, similarly to the *anamnesis* of creation, in constant dialogue between within and without. In contrast to the presumption of gnostic teachers who wanted to convince the faithful that their naive faith must be understood and applied much differently, John could say: you do not need such instruction, as anointed ones (baptized ones) you know everything (cf. 1 John 2:20). This does not mean a factual omniscience on the part of the faithful. It does signify, however, the sureness of the Christian memory. This Christian memory, to be sure, is always learning, but proceeding from its sacramental identity, it also distinguishes from within between what is a genuine unfolding of its recollection and what is its destruction or falsification. In the crisis of church today, the power of this recollection and the truth of the apostolic word is experienced in an entirely new way, where much more so than hierarchical direction, it is the power of memory of the simple faith which leads to the discernment of spirits. One can only comprehend the primacy of the pope and its correlation to Christian conscience in this connection. The true sense of the teaching authority of the pope consists in his being the advocate of the Christian memory. The pope does not impose from without. Rather he elucidates the Christian memory and defends it. For this reason the toast to conscience indeed must precede the toast to the pope because without conscience there would not be a papacy. All power that the papacy has is power of conscience. It is service to the double memory upon which the faith is based and which again and again must be purified, expanded, and defended against the destruction of memory which is threatened by a subjectivity forgetful of its own foundation as well as by the pressures of social and cultural conformity.

b) Conscientia

Having considered this first, essentially ontological, level of the concept of conscience, we must now turn to its second level, that of judgment and decision which the medieval tradition designates with the single word *conscientia*, conscience. Presumably this terminological tradition has not insignificantly contributed to the diminution of the concept of conscience. Thomas, for example, only designates this second level as *conscientia*. For him it stands to reason that conscience is not a *habitus*, that is, a lasting ontic quality of man, but *actus*, an event in execution. Thomas of course assumes as given the ontological foundation of *anamnesis* (*synderesis*). He describes *anamnesis* as an inner repugnance to evil and an attraction to the good. The act of conscience applies this basic knowledge to the particular situation. It is divided according to Thomas into three elements: recognizing (*recognoscere*), bearing witness (*tesificari*), and finally judging (*iudicare*). One might speak of an interaction between a function of control and a function of decision.[16] Thomas sees this sequence according to the Aristotelian tradition's model of deductive reasoning. But he is careful to emphasize what is peculiar to this knowledge of moral actions whose conclusions do not come from mere knowing or thinking.[17] Whether something is recognized or not depends too on the will which can block the way to recognition or lead to it. It is dependent, that is to say, on an already formed moral character which can either continue to deform or be further purified.[18] On this level, the level of judgment (*conscientia* in the narrower sense), it can be said that even the erroneous conscience binds. This statement is completely intelligible from the rational tradition of scholasticism. No one may act against his convictions, as St. Paul had already said (Romans 14:23). But the fact that the conviction a person has come to certainly binds in the moment of acting does not signify a canonization of subjectivity. It is never wrong to follow the convictions one has arrived at—in fact, one must do so. But it can very well be wrong to have come to such askew convictions in the first place by having stifled the protest of the *anamnesis* of being. The guilt lies then in a different place, much deeper—not in the present act, not in the present judgment of conscience, but in the neglect of my being which made me deaf to the internal promptings of truth.[19] For this reason, criminals of conviction like Hitler and Stalin are guilty. These crass examples should not serve to put us at ease but should rouse us to take seriously the earnestness of the plea: "Free me from my unknown guilt" (Psalm 19:13).

Epilogue: Conscience and Grace

At the end there remains the question with which we began. Is not the truth, at least as the faith of the church shows it to us, too lofty and difficult for man? Taking into consideration everything we have said,

we can respond as follows. Certainly, the high road to truth and goodness is not a comfortable one. It challenges man. Nevertheless, retreat
into self, however comfortable, does not redeem. The self withers
away and becomes lost. But in ascending the heights of the good, man
discovers more and more the beauty which lies in the arduousness of
truth which constitutes redemption for him. But not everything has
yet been said. We would dissolve Christianity into moralism if no
message which surpasses our own actions became discernible. Without many words an image from the Greek world can show us this. In
it we can observe simultaneously both how the *anamnesis* of the creator extends from within us outward toward the redeemer, and how
everyone may see him as redeemer, because he answers our own
innermost expectations. I am speaking of the story of the expiation of
the sin of the matricide of Orestes. He had committed the murder as
an act of conscience. This is designated by the mythological language
of obedience to the command of the god Apollo. But now he finds
himself hounded by the furies or *erinyes*, who are to be seen as mythological personifications of conscience which, from a deeper wellspring
of recollection, reproach Orestes, declaring that his decision of conscience, his obedience to the "saying of the gods," was in reality guilt.
The whole tragedy of man comes to light in this dispute of the "gods,"
that is to say, in this conflict of conscience. In the holy court, the white
stone of Athena leads to Orestes's acquittal, his sanctification of the
power by which the *erinyes* are transformed into *eumenides*, the spirits
of reconciliation. Atonement has transformed the world. The myth,
while representing the transition from a system of blood vengeance to
the right order of community, signifies much more than just that. Hans
Urs von Balthasar expressed this "more" as follows: "Calming grace
always assists in the establishing of justice, not the old graceless justice of the Erinyes period, but that which is full of grace."[20] This myth
speaks to us of the human longing that conscience's objectively just
indictment and the attendant destructive, interior distress it causes in
man, not be the last word. It thus speaks of an authority of grace, a
power of expiation which allows the guilt to vanish and makes truth
at last truly redemptive. It is the longing for a truth which does not just
make demands of us but also transforms us through expiation and pardon. Through these, as Aeschylus puts it, "guilt is washed away"[21] and
our being is transformed from within, beyond our own capability. This

is the real innovation of Christianity. The Logos, the truth in person, is also the atonement, the transforming forgiveness above and beyond our capability and incapability. Therein lies the real novelty upon which the larger Christian memory is founded and which indeed, at the same time, constitutes the deeper answer to what the *anamnesis* of the creator expects of us. Where this center of the Christian message is not sufficiently expressed and appreciated, truth becomes a yoke which is too heavy for our shoulders and from which we must seek to free ourselves. But the freedom gained thereby is empty. It leads into the desolate land of nothingness and disintegrates of itself. Yet the yoke to truth in fact became "easy" (Matthew 11:30) when the truth came, loved us, and consumed our guilt in the fire of his love. Only when we know and experience this from within will we be free to hear the message of conscience with joy and without fear.

Notes

1. This thesis was apparently first proposed by J. G. Fichte; "Conscience does not and cannot err," because it is "itself judge of all conviction," which "recognizes no higher judge over itself. It is the ultimate authority and cannot be appealed" (*System der Sittenlehre*, 1798, III, 15; Werke Bd. 4, Berlin 1971, p. 174). Cf. H. Reiner, *Gewissen*, in: J. Ritter (ed.), *Historisches Wörterbuch der Philosophie III*, p. 574-592, here p. 586. Kant had already previously formulated the counterarguments. They appear in more depth in Hegel for whom conscience "as formal subjectivity . . . (is) always on the verge of changing into evil." Cf. H. Reiner, ibid. Nevertheless, the thesis of the infallibility of conscience is at present again in the ascendancy in popular theological literature. I find a—in a certain respect—mediating position in E. Schockenhoff, *Das umstrittene Gewissen* (Mainz, 1990), which expressly reckons with the possibility that conscience can miss its mark by going astray of the other requirement of the moral law, the mutual recognition of the free rational being (p. 139). Schockenhoff, however—relying on Linsenmann—rejects talk of an erring conscience: "In view of the quality of conscience as such, there is no sense in speaking of error because there is no higher observation point from which error could be ascertained" (p. 136). Why not? Is there no truth concerning the good accessible to all of us in common? To be sure, the point is then so significantly nuanced that finally in the end it is even less clear to me why the concept of the erring conscience should be untenable. Helpful here is M. Honecker's *Einführung in die theologische Ethik*. Berlin, 1990. pp. 138ff.

2. A. Görres, "Schuld und Schuldgefühle," in *Internationale katholische Zeitschrift "Communio"* 13 (1984), p. 434.

3. Ibid., p. 442.

4. Cf. M. Honecker, op. cit. (cf. Note 1), p. 130.

5. Besides the important article already cited of H. Reiner and the work of Schockenhoff on new studies, cf. A. Laun, *Das Gewissen: Oberste Norm sittlichen Handelns* (Innsbruck, 1984) and his *Aktuelle Probleme der Moraltheologie* (Vienna, 1991), pp. 31-64; J. Gründel (ed.), *Das Gewissen: Subjektive Willkür oder oberste Norm?* (Düsseldorf, 1990); summary overview: K. Golser, "Gewissen," in H. Rotter, G. Virt, *Neues Lexikon der christlichen Moral* (Innsbruck, Vienna, 1990), pp. 278-286.

6. Letter of Norfolk, in *Works of Cardinal Newman: Difficulties of Anglicans II* (Westminster, Maryland: Christian Classics, 1969), p. 261; cf. J. Honoré, *Newman; Sa Vie et sa Pensée* (Paris, 1988), p. 65; I. Ker: *J. H. Newman, A Biography* (Oxford, 1990), pp. 688ff.

7. Cf. Ch. St. Dessian, *J. H. Newman* (Oxford Univ. Press, 3rd ed., 1980); G. Biemer, *J. H. Newman: Leben und Werk* (Mainz, 1989).

8. From the famous poem "Lead Kindly Light" in *Verses on Various Occasions* (London, 1888); cf. Ker, op. cit., p. 79; cf. Dessain, op. cit., pp. 33-34.

9. Letter to J. Keble of Dec. 29, 1844 in *Correspondence of J. H. Newman with J. Keble and Others: 1839-1845* (London, 1917), p. 364, cf. also p. 351; cf. Dessain, op. cit., p. 79.

10. Cf. P. Berglar, *Die Stunde des Thomas Morus* (Olten and Freiburg, 3rd ed., 1981), pp. 155ff.

11. Regarding the debate between Socrates and the Sophists, cf. J. Pieper, "Missbrauch der Sprache–Missbrauch der Macht," In *Über die Schwierigkeit zu glauben* (Munich, 1974), pp. 255-282 and *Kümmert euch nicht um Sokrates* (Munich, 1966). A penetrating treatment of the question of the truth as the center of Socratic searching is found in R. Guardini, *The Death of Socrates* (New York: Sheed and Ward, 1948).

12. A short summary of the medieval doctrine of conscience can be found in H. Reiner, op. cit., (cf. Note 1), pp. 582f.

13. Cf. E. von Ivánka, *Plato christianus* (Einsiedeln, 1964), pp. 315-351, esp. pp. 320f.

14. *Regulae fusius tractatae* Resp 2, 1 PG 31, 908.

15. *De trin VIII* 3, 4 PL 42, 949.

16. Cf. H. Reiner, op. cit., p. 582: *Summa Theologica* I, q. 79 a 13; *De Ver.* q. 17 a 1.

17. Cf. the careful study of L. Melina, *La conoscenza morale: Linee di riflessione sul Commento di san Tommaso all 'Etica Nicomachea* (Rome: Città Nuova Editrice, 1987), pp. 69ff.

18. In reflecting on his own inner experience in the decades following his conversion, St. Augustine elaborated fundamental insights into the essence of freedom and morality concerning the relationships between knowledge, will, emotion, and inclination through habit. Cf. the excellent presentation of P. Brown, *Augustine of Hippo: A Biography* (New York: Dorset, 1986), pp. 146-157.

19. That this precisely is also the position of St. Thomas Aquinas is shown by I. G. Belmans in his extremely enlightening study "Le paradoxe de la conscience erronée d' Abélard à Karl Rahner" in *Rev Thom* 90 (1990), pp. 570-586. He shows how with the publication of Sertillanges's book on St. Thomas in 1942 a then widely adopted distortion of Thomas's doctrine of conscience takes hold which–to put it simply–consists in the fact that only the *Summa Theologica* I-II, q. 19 a 5 ("Must one follow an erroneous conscience?") is cited and the following article 6 ("Is it sufficient to follow one's conscience in order to act properly?") is simply ignored. That means imputing the doctrine of Abelard to Thomas whose goal was in fact to overcome Abelard. Abelard had taught that the crucifiers of Christ would not have sinned if they had acted from ignorance. The only way to sin consists in acting against conscience. The modern theories of the autonomy of conscience can appeal to Abelard but not to Thomas.

20. H. U. v. Balthasar, *Glory of the Lord: A Theological Aesthetics IV: The Realm of Metaphysics in Antiquity* (San Francisco: Ignatius Press, 1989), p. 121.

21. Aeschylus, *Eumenides* 280-282 (Oxford edition, G. Murray, 2nd ed., 1955); Balthasar, op. cit., p. 121.

2

Crisis of Conscience and Culture

JOHN M. HAAS

The world is living through a period of moral crisis. It can perhaps be characterized more specifically as a crisis of conscience, since conscience constitutes the ability of man to judge right from wrong. As Pope John Paul II indicates in *Evangelium Vitae*, today "conscience itself (is) darkened ... finding it increasingly difficult to distinguish between good and evil."[1] The pope warns that we are faced with "an extremely serious and mortal danger: that of confusion between good and evil." And in his encyclical *Veritatis Splendor* he warns of "a headlong plunge into the most dangerous crisis which can afflict man: the confusion between good and evil, which makes it impossible to build up and to preserve the moral order of individuals and communities."[2]

Since conscience is the ability to make judgments about what is truly good and what is evil, a loss of that capacity can only mean eventual disaster in personal or social life. A darkening of the conscience means a diminishing of our very humanity. John Henry Newman considered conscience to be an irrefutable component of the make-up of the human person, an undeniable capacity of man's psyche:

> I assume, then, that Conscience has a legitimate place among our mental acts; as really so, as the action of memory, of reasoning, of imagination, or as the sense of the beautiful; that, as there are objects which, when presented to the mind, cause it to feel grief, regret, joy, or desire, so there are things which excite in us approbation or blame,

and which we in consequence call right or wrong; and which, experienced in ourselves, kindle in us that specific sense of pleasure or
pain, which goes by the name of a good or bad conscience.[3]

The loss of this capacity can be as disastrous to the moral life as the
loss of the sense of touch can be to one's physical existence. When the
sense of touch is lost or diminished, an individual is vastly more vul-
nerable to life-threatening injury. For example, the warning signal of
pain will no longer be communicated when a hand is placed on a hot
stove. Analogously, when conscience is diminished or lost, an individual is in another kind of mortal danger. Without the accusatory
pain of conscience when one is contemplating an evil act, one may
not be restrained from a morally injurious deed.

Yet there seem to be increased reports of the dulling of this perfected ability to judge between right and wrong. Indeed, appeal to
private conscience is the way in which the widespread destruction of
fetal life is most often defended today, and the way in which arguments for euthanasia are being advanced. No one wants to say that he
or she is acting in any way other than conscientiously, despite the fact
that individuals will perform actions that in the past would have received universal moral condemnation.

John Paul II points out that the modern understanding of conscience
as that which confirms our subjective desires rather than the means of
discovering objective truth and acting upon it is one of the principal
causes of our current moral crisis. In *Dominum et Vivificantem* the pope
reminds his readers that "conscience is not an independent and exclusive capacity to decide what is good and what is evil."[4] Conscience is
not the power to determine what is good, but to recognize what is good
and to choose accordingly. The pope stresses this capacity of the conscience "to read" reality. The authority and the judgments of conscience
"derive from the truth about moral good and evil, which [the conscience]
is called to listen to and to express. . . . The judgment of conscience
does not establish the [moral] law; rather it bears witness [to it]."[5]

A number of years ago a statue was erected in England to the honor
of St. Thomas More. At the ceremonies there were prelatial representatives not only of the Catholic Church but of the Anglican Church as
well. In such an ecumenical setting the virtues manifested by Sir Thomas More had to be enumerated rather delicately so as not to offend

the sensibilities of the successors of those who had put him to death. To erect such a statue in the pluralistic society of today's England meant speakers had to address those attributes of More's that contemporary English Anglicans, Catholics, and even secularists admired. In the ceremonies, therefore, More was referred to as "a martyr to conscience."

This appellation refers, of course, to More's integrity and fortitude in the face of persecution. But I imagine St. Thomas would have found the title odd and would have commented on its oddity with his characteristic wit. St. Thomas More was not a martyr, that is, "witness," to conscience, but rather to the truth, to the true Faith, to the Catholic Church, to the person of Christ and his vicar. St. Thomas More uncompromisingly clung to, not a capacity to make sound moral judgments, but rather to the good, which he prized above all else. Conscience could hand him no crown of life. His heavenly Father could.

After he was condemned to death, More penned a prayer for his enemies as he sat imprisoned in the Tower of London. He prayed that God would make both his enemies and him "saved souls in heaven together, where we may ever live and love together with You and Your blessed saints. O glorious Trinity, grant this for the sake of the bitter passion of our sweet Savior Christ."

More himself partook of the "bitter passion" of the "sweet Savior" to whom he bore witness. He had indeed acted on conscience, but it was a conscience that had rightly judged the truth of the matter: the king was not, nor could he ever be, head of the Church of England. More's son-in-law Roper witnessed the execution. He said Sir Thomas complied with the king's wish that he not speak at length to the crowd. "Wherefore," wrote Roper, "briefly he desired all the people to pray for him and to bear witness with him that he there died in and for the faith of the Holy Catholic Church."[6]

St. Thomas More was faithful to his conscience and therefore was a martyr, not to it, but to truth, indeed to the Truth Incarnate and his church.

Crisis of Culture

The crisis of conscience today is much more than the inability of individuals to make sound moral judgments. In *Evangelium Vitae* the pope indicated that the moral disorder today is indeed a "crisis of culture."[7] It can be characterized as a cultural crisis because the failure of conscience is seen not simply in wicked men choosing to embrace evil in pursuit of their own selfish interests, but rather in the attempt of entire societies to forge their common life without recourse to objective standards of right and wrong.

This is a most alarming development, since, as the pope writes, "the dignity of the human person has its foundation in the conscience."[8] Conscience is the font of man's dominion and moral grandeur and so is "the monitor of true social and moral order."[9]

Since individuals have ceased to understand conscience as the capacity to make sound moral judgments in conformity with the truth, we are faced with a cultural crisis of the gravest moment. Cultures are shaped by the way in which conscientious men, women, and children make daily decisions about issues of great and little significance.

Individuals are likewise shaped, molded, in some respects, constituted by their culture. They receive their understanding of themselves and their world from the conversation and ritual of the kitchen table; the rough and tumble of the playing field; the hierarchies, rewards, and punishments of the classroom; the annual military parade; the language of the streets; the Saturday night dance; the Sunday morning liturgy. Understandings of men and women, marriage and family, honor and treachery, are drawn from the very cultural air they breathe. Most of this is unconsciously received and shapes them interiorly.

We could perhaps speak of certain "cultural coordinates" that enable us to live successfully in society. In mathematics, coordinates are any of the magnitudes that define the position of a point or a line by reference to a fixed figure. Coordinates serve a similar role in sailing. The sailor takes his coordinates from the fixed night sky so that he may navigate successfully to his destination. Likewise, there are certain "cultural coordinates," certain ideas and concepts that seem fixed in society. One does not call them into question because one could not imagine navigating one's way through life without them. The problem is that many of these "coordinates" or cultural presuppositions are incompatible with a sound philosophical anthropology. And without a sound anthropology there can be no dependable doctrine of conscience.

From the beginning of his pontificate, John Paul II has been very sensitive to what might be called "the cultural issue." Early in his reign, the pope established the Pontifical Council for Culture to assist the church in her dialogue with contemporary cultures. In virtually all his encyclicals he has called, not just for the conversion of souls, but for the evangelization or re-evangelization of culture. The pope knows the cultural milieu will facilitate or hinder, indeed almost nullify, all efforts at the conversion of individual persons. He has spoken of the deformation of conscience that can result from a disordered environment: "It happens not infrequently in history, for more or less lengthy periods and under the influence of different factors, that the moral conscience of many people becomes seriously clouded. 'Have we the right idea of conscience?' . . . 'Is it not true that modern man is threatened with an eclipse of conscience? By a deformation of conscience? By a numbness or deadening of conscience?'"[10]

We can see vividly in our day the coarsening of culture and desensitizing of the communal conscience. An older woman told me of a homily she had heard just after the Second World War. She was a young woman and beginning to make her way in the world. In the sermon the priest warned of social trends in the United States (this was the late 1940s) and said that if they continued the day might be reached when even abortion might become commonplace. She told me how stunned she was by the priest's use of the word *abortion* and said that the mere mention of the word in the homily made her slightly nauseated.

Today, however, people can look on photographs of the dismembered bodies of unborn babies killed by dilation and curettage or the burned, red bodies of perfectly formed children killed by saline abortions and not even be moved. The conscience of entire societies has been dangerously dulled in our day.

Pope John Paul II is quite clear that the crisis of culture is particularly far advanced in the "developed" countries. None of his writings has reached the intensity of concern with the cultural problem of conscience as does *Evangelium Vitae*, in which the pope contrasts the culture of life with the "culture of death," which is advancing above all in the prosperous societies of the world.[11]

In *Evangelium Vitae*, the pope uses extremely harsh language to describe the contemporary moral climate and speaks of societies reverting "to a state of barbarism,"[12] of "scientifically and systematically programmed threats (to life),"[13] of "an objective conspiracy against life,"[14] and of "crimes against life,"[15] much of it being the "sinister result of a relativism which reigns unopposed."[16] It is a time of "the most alarming corruption and the darkest moral blindness."[17]

It is a very bleak social picture the pope presents. "In the background," writes the pope, "there is the profound crisis of culture, which generates skepticism in relation to the very foundations of knowledge and ethics, and which makes it increasingly difficult to grasp clearly the meaning of what man is, the meaning of his rights and duties."[18]

This cultural confusion is not confined to secular culture alone. It has also infected the church herself.

The question of dissent from certain authoritative magisterial moral doctrines is today not merely a matter of disagreeing with this or that particular doctrine or moral norm. The very understanding of the human person that the church has always taught is now called into question. In the exercise of his conscience, man is now presented as the arbiter of truth rather than the discoverer of it. The Holy Father has been very direct about this. He writes in *Veritatis Splendor*, "It is no longer a matter of limited and occasional dissent, but of an overall and systematic calling into question of traditional moral doctrine, on the basis of certain anthropological and ethical presuppositions. At the root of the presuppositions is the more or less obvious influence of currents of thought which end by detaching human freedom from its essential and constitutive relationship to truth."[19]

Unless these presuppositions are addressed, it seems the attempt on the part of the church to address dissenters on contraception or abortion or homosexuality will of necessity be unsuccessful. Individuals will continue to appeal to contemporary society's disordered understanding of conscience to justify their actions. They will appeal to conscience as the power to forge truth itself and to depart from the wisdom of received morality. They interpret James Russell Lowell's lines as relativists: "New occasions teach new duties, time makes ancient truth uncouth."[20] The church's arguments will not even be heard. The moral language used to put them forward derives from a different culture with different anthropological presuppositions. And even if the arguments are heard, they will not be understood.

Some Erroneous Cultural Presuppositions
and Their Origins

The pope identifies in several of his writings what some of these cultural and anthropological presuppositions are. He speaks of subjectivism, relativism, a belief in the absolute autonomy and unrestrained freedom of the individual, consumerism, hedonism, skepticism. Anyone who has received a liberal education today knows that the ones who have shaped modern culture are the likes of Luther, Calvin, Bacon, Newton, Descartes, Rousseau, Voltaire, Kant, Leibniz, Fichte, Hegel, Schopenhauer, Nietzsche, Hume, Locke, Hobbes, Bentham, Mill, Darwin, Freud, Marx, Engels, Lenin, Jefferson, James, and Dewey.[21] In his book of very personal reflections, *Crossing the Threshold of Hope*,[22] the pope mentions the thought of a number of these men as contributing to the subjectivism and relativism of our day. And not one of these shapers of contemporary culture could be said to have had an anthropology consistent with Catholic doctrine, which teaches that man is rational and free and capable of noble and meritorious acts despite his proclivity toward evil. Man must also be understood as created, which means his very being is ordered toward intelligible ends or goals so that true freedom consists in choosing actions that are compatible with his ends and will help him attain them.

Kantianism

One of the principal cultural presuppositions of our day, which the pope mentions as a hindrance to a sound doctrine on conscience, is the view that human freedom is absolutely autonomous and subjective. One can recognize here the influence of Immanuel Kant, who insisted that man can be truly moral only if he is absolutely free, not only from external constraints and pressures, but, in a sense, even from his own body. Kant believed that any form of heteronomy, or law imposed from without, would violate man's freedom and result in the destruction of morality. In determining the morality of an act one does not, for example, look even to the natural inclinations of the body and the ends toward which these inclinations are ordered, because this would constitute heteronomy, a coercion exercised over the agent by someone or something other than his own intellect and will. If one were to follow his inclinations, how would he know he were truly free? And freedom is the hallmark of morality. The only motive one can have for the moral act is that of a sense of duty, of obligation.

According to Kant, the moral agent "regards himself as determinable only through laws which he gives himself through reason."[23] This absolute autonomy requires the subject to articulate the moral law for himself. For Kant, the moral law would not be different for each person, since human nature is the same in all, and the moral law that one formulates for oneself must be universalizable. But, in a sense, nothing stands higher than the moral law and the individual who articulates it for himself. Even the existence of God, human freedom, and the immortality of the soul are postulates of the moral law. Because, for example, the obligations of the moral law cannot be fully realized in this life, and because one cannot have an obligation without the possibility of fulfilling it, there must be life after death. In such a manner Kant argues for the immortality of the soul–and human freedom and the existence of God. But none of these could be conceived apart from the moral law, which is known directly. Even Jesus Christ himself and the truth of his gospel must be subjected to the canons of autonomous, universalizable morality. As Kant writes, "Even the holy One of the Gospel himself must first of all be measured against our ideal of moral perfection before one acknowledges him as such."[24]

For Kant, the individual becomes the creator of reality and morality. Kant held it impossible for the mind ultimately to come to know reality as "raw fact." The mind cannot attain "*das Ding an sich,*" "the thing itself," the "noumenon." All that can be known are the "phenomena" or inchoate sense data upon which the mind imposes its construct of reality through its innate categories. And the subject is also entirely the creator of the moral law. As one of his followers put it, in Kant we see "the conquest of the metaphysics of being, the transfer of the center of gravity from the object to the subject."[25] There is no longer an objective order "out there," which can be known and used as a guide to human behavior. It seems that John Paul II is firmly determined to attempt the transfer of the center of gravity from the subject back to the object, which is to say, God's created order.

Kant would not have viewed himself as a subjectivist or a relativist, of course. But he has been supremely influential in modern philosophy, and his insistence on the absolute autonomy and freedom of the individual has contributed greatly to the rise of subjectivism and relativism. One can see the influence of Kant even in Catholic moral theology. It is present, for example, in the idea of the transcendental freedom of the fundamental option proposed by certain Catholic moral theologians, which the pope in *Veritatis Splendor* judged to constitute a danger to sound moral doctrine. According to the proponents of the fundamental option, the moral agent enjoys a "transcendental" freedom that is not constrained by particular, concrete circumstances. In a sense, one becomes so autonomous in the formal ethics of Kant and his followers that one is free of concrete reality. And with the theory of the fundamental option, one becomes virtually free of the consequences of individual, concrete moral acts as one remains fundamentally ordered to God by virtue of an act of one's transcendental freedom. Mortal sin as a concrete possibility becomes almost impossible.

There are obviously many other sources for the pervasive subjectivism and moral relativism of our day, but Kant certainly remains one of the principal ones. Kant, of course, tried to reconcile the claims of narrow rationalism on the one hand with empiricism on the other. He wanted to avoid Humean skepticism, and to establish mechanistic Newtonian physics on the one hand and subjective Rousseauvian morality on the other. He was not successful. The reconciliation was not achieved. One of the contradictions inherent in Kant's approach is that he ends up attributing a complete freedom to the interior man but a necessity to his physical existence that allows no freedom.

In *Veritatis Splendor* the pope speaks of appeals to this unchecked and unrestrained freedom postulated by Kant. He writes, "Freedom would thus lay claim to a moral autonomy which would actually amount to an absolute sovereignty."[26] But the pope also seems to see in current trends in moral theory the paradox in Kant's philosophical anthropology of an absolute freedom noumenally and determinism phenomenally. "Side by side with its exaltation of freedom, yet oddly in contrast with it," the pope writes, "modern culture radically questions the very existence of this freedom. . . . Some people have come to question or even deny the very reality of human freedom."[27]

In this context, the pope makes reference to certain approaches to the behavioral sciences that deny man's freedom and hence his true nature. It is interesting to note that the title of the book by the behaviorist B. F. Skinner fully acknowledges the intrinsic relationship between freedom and human dignity. Skinner entitled his book *Beyond Freedom and Dignity*. But, of course, the Christian John Paul II locates man's dignity precisely in his freedom, which is of the divine image within him.

Certain Elements in Protestant Thought

While we often look to the philosophers and chroniclers of culture in the seventeenth and eighteenth centuries as laying the foundations for contemporary culture, it would be well not to ignore the influence of sixteenth-century Protestantism, for it has had a profound impact on our contemporary understanding of conscience. For example, it should not be forgotten that Kant himself was formed in the context of Prussian Pietistic Protestantism.

The wealthy, powerful nations of the West today are predominantly shaped by a Protestant or secularist outlook. Some of the tenets of classical Protestantism are precursors of many of the erroneous cultural presuppositions of our own day.

The doctrine of the total depravity of man, for example, led to a denigration of the role of reason in charting a moral path for oneself. Reason was not to be trusted. Indeed, it could pose a threat to salvation by leading man to the deadly sin of pride. Reason was, Luther declared, the devil's whore. In *Commentary on Galatians* Luther wrote that "every Christian is a true priest; for first he offers up and kills his own reason. . . . The evening sacrifice is to kill reason."[28]

For classical Protestantism, judgments of conscience are not to be trusted. Hebrews 9:14 will sometimes be interpreted to mean that even the conscience is unclean.[29] If conscience is fundamentally a judgment of the intellect about whether a contemplated action is good or bad, and if reason itself is totally corrupt and not to be trusted, then conscience cannot be trusted. Since fallen man cannot perform any action that is good and meritorious in the sight of God, he must simply act as he thinks best, realizing that his action will still be tainted with sin, and throw himself on God's mercy.

There is a way in which reflections on whether a conscience is correct or incorrect are irrelevant in such a system. One cannot know what is truly good; it is not necessary to know what is truly good; and so one acts in ignorance and sin relying on God's grace.

Calvin's doctrine on double predestination and Luther's treatise *The Bondage of the Will*, which deny any role to the human will in salvation, have contributed to the extremes of both determinism and absolute freedom as they are often manifested in contemporary culture. If one is saved by grace alone without any human cooperation, and if all actions are tainted with sin, one can simply, as Luther put it, "sin boldly."[30]

Also, the Protestant principle of *sola scriptura* linked to a belief in the private interpretation of scripture surely was, and continues to be, a powerful impetus toward the widespread subjectivism of our day. This doctrine is sometimes known as the "internal testimony of the Holy Spirit." The *Westminster Confession* states succinctly: "Our full persuasion and assurance of the infallible truth and divine authority [of scripture], is from the inward work of the Holy Spirit bearing witness by and with the Word in our hearts."[31]

A Calvinist would reject the idea that the inner conviction which a believer has is *merely* a subjective feeling. The feeling is, as it were, the result of the inner conviction. But the danger of subjectivism can hardly be minimized. Calvin described this inner assurance as "a conviction that requires no reasons."[32] Without "reasons" there is no role for reason. Protestants have always made appeal to the certitude they have interiorly of the convictions they hold, even when these convictions separate them from the testimony and fellowship of other Christians—and indeed the entire Christian tradition that has preceded them. They allow of no authority other than their own to judge the correctness or error of their beliefs. The Catholic avoids subjectivism by always receiving his beliefs from the community of faith and by having his interpretation of scripture measured against the common faith of the community and the authoritative teaching of the magisterium.

While Catholics happily recognize the faith shared with those of other ecclesial communities, there must still be a willingness to consider the Protestant contributions to the erroneous cultural presuppositions of our day. Protestant doctrines such as total depravity, double predestination, *sola scriptura, sola gratia, sola fides,* the sinner as *simul justus et peccator,* the denigration of reason and exaltation of the will, have all contributed to the subjectivism, individualism, emotivism, belief in absolute autonomy, and the rebellion against authority that have shaped the way in which conscience is understood in contemporary Western culture.

Totalitarianism

Totalitarianism has been another major cultural phenomenon giving distinctive shape to our century. Totalitarianism has posed an unspeakably grave threat to the dignity of the human person in this century and has exerted its own influence on the notion of conscience.

Conscience implies human freedom, the very kind of freedom the totalitarians of our day have been quick to try to suppress. But it was not mere misanthropy on the part of the totalitarians that led them to do this! Within the framework of their own terribly disordered theories, they thought they were deeply committed to the good of humanity. Their ideology usually involved a false anthropology and hence a false idea of freedom. After all, the Nazis did have signs welcoming prisoners to their camps: *"Arbeit macht frei."* "Work liberates."

The totalitarianism of National Socialism believed that it was advancing the good of humanity by purifying it of races or ethnic groups that would impede its biological advance and ultimate perfection. The totalitarian state of Marxism-Leninism believed that it was but a necessary stage in the inexorable movement of history toward the classless society of the future, when the state itself would wither away. This forward movement was accomplished through the necessary and unavoidable brutality of the class struggle. In either socialist system, that of Nazism or Communism, there was truly no role for conscience, because in either system man was not perceived as being truly free. The only real choice that lay before one was to cast one's lot with the forces of history. The only judgment to be made about a given act was whether or not it advanced the revolution or the race. In such systems there was no place for moral absolutes, which themselves would challenge the absolutism of the state.

Virtually any act became permissible, indeed perhaps even obligatory, if it helped move humanity toward its goal. Human nature certainly did not serve as a guide in formulating moral judgments, since human nature was an unfinished project. The Marxists spoke of our being "artisans of humanity," of being our own creators. Here again one encounters the notion of absolute autonomy on the part of man, but in this case it is "communal man" rather than "individual man." There are simply no bounds to the exercise of his Promethean will.

Such ideas came to be highly influential even within the Catholic Church in the liberation theology movement. The authors within this movement attempted to apply Marxist analysis to the contemporary social and economic order, and they imbued Catholic theological categories with new meaning. Gustavo Gutiérrez wrote: "To announce the Gospel is to proclaim that the love of God is present in the historical becoming of mankind."[33] Elsewhere he wrote: "To build a just society today necessarily implies the active and conscious participation in the class struggle that is occurring before our eyes."[34] Here one can clearly see the influence of Marxist ideology and its conviction that mankind advances inexorably in history through the class struggle.

When the Holy See wanted to address the errors contained in liberation theology, it was faced with a delicate task. There were many who considered themselves to be liberation theologians or members of that movement who had virtually no awareness of the influence of Marxist ideology. These people were convinced that liberation theology was a trustworthy approach to social analysis and praxis. They merely wanted to advance the concerns of the poor and the dispossessed in conformity with the teaching of the gospel. In my opinion, the Holy See wanted to address the basic dangerous concepts contained within liberation theology without actually denouncing the movement as such, thereby creating consternation, confusion, and perhaps even alienation from the church among the movement's followers who were acting in good faith. This is why, I believe, the Holy See never explicitly condemned liberation theology. However, the Congregation for the Doctrine of the Faith issued two *Instructions* on liberation theology;

these repudiated the central philosophical theses without which liberation theology could not hold together as a coherent system.[35]

These two documents are significant for the discussion of conscience because of their repudiation of an ideology advancing a socioeconomic system that would deny individual responsibility for actions. An individual was either for or against the advance of history, according to the Marxists, but it was the proletariate class that was the driving force of history, not the individual. And the outcome of the historical process was inevitable. There was not true freedom of action. How could this constitute liberation?

To be liberated from a supposed oppression by the bourgeoisie, which would inevitably happen no matter what one did individually, was an ephemeral liberation. But not only do the *Instructions* repudiate the false analyses and claims of Marxist ideology, they also caution against any such ideas being used in Catholic thought. Both documents insist that true liberation for man is to be set free from sin rather than set free from impersonal social structures such as the Marxists argued. The *Instructions* argued against a political culture that fundamentally denied human freedom. And without freedom there is no role for conscience. Any such doctrines working their way into Catholic thought would vitiate the Christian message itself and nullify the work of Christ in the lives of those who might adopt it.

Whether one is dealing with the false cultural presuppositions of secularist consumerism and its bourgeois moral theology of proportionalism or dealing with socialism and its radical theology of liberation, one finds at the heart a false anthropology. They do not know the truth about man as a created being with a set nature that must be acknowledged and that can serve as a guide for the work of conscience. The cultural presuppositions of absolute autonomy and freedom, on the one hand, or determinism on the other are challenges to Catholic truth, which means that they are also challenges to the truth about man as rational and free.

From the beginning of his pontificate John Paul II has tried to restate the truth about man so as to bring philosophical reflection about man and the social policies based on such reflection back to a sense of reverence for man. When the truth about man is known, respect for him and his rights naturally follows. John Paul II speaks of man with a sense of wonder and indeed veneration. "With what veneration must the apostle of Christ utter this word, man," the pope declared at his inaugural mass. He has seen and experienced firsthand the unspeakable crimes committed against man by both the Nazis and the Communists in this century. He has seen the defeat of both these totalitarian systems, having himself made a significant, personal contribution to the overthrow of East European Communism. But the flowering of a new Christian humanism has not occurred. Instead the pope has had to watch new threats to man arise within the context of the liberal democracies, threats that have in some respects proven to be no less grave than they were under totalitarianism. Because of the wealth and efficiency of the liberal democracies, the threats have not been as obvious, as direct, and as vulgar as they were under Fascism or Communism. Consequently, they have a greater and more subtle and hence more dangerous allure.

Because the utilitarian democracies increasingly fail to see and understand the truth about man as creature made in the image and likeness of God, they see him as the raw material for their own creating, as had been the case also with the totalitarians. If a given individual is useless, either for social productivity or for someone's gratification, he is expendable. He has no intrinsic worth. Value is bestowed upon him or withdrawn from him on the whim of those who have power in a utilitarian democracy. Consequently, the pope says, such a democracy has itself now been transformed into "a *tyrant state* which arrogates to itself the right to dispose of the life of the weakest and most defenseless members, from the unborn child to the elderly, in the name of public interest which is really nothing but the interest of one part."[36] An appeal to majority decision by such democracies constitutes nothing but a "tragic caricature of legality," for if such societies do not acknowledge and safeguard the dignity of each person, they have betrayed the democratic ideal in its very foundations. The state can bestow worth on no one. Each person's incomparable worth has been bestowed by God, who has created man in his own image. The state can only acknowledge this dignity of man and then is obliged to formulate policies that protect, safeguard, and promote it. When the political system is no longer guided by such truths, "acts of conscience" by individual representatives of it can actually work against the good of man and constitute grave threats to his well-being and even his life.

Crisis of Religion

At the very depths of the crisis of conscience and of culture today, there is a crisis of religion. It is, after all, religion that most profoundly shapes a culture; indeed, it is *cultus* or worship from which culture derives.

We speak here not of a crisis of faith but of religion. Faith is a supernatural gift given by God to men through the transforming power of sanctifying grace. Faith is the possession of those alone to whom it has been given. Religion, on the other hand, is the natural virtue, common to all men, by which they acknowledge God as Creator and themselves as dependent creatures. Without an awareness of mankind and the world as *creatura*, there can be no awareness of an objective, intelligible order providing the basis for an objective morality, because this cosmic order is derived from the creative act of God.

Religion belongs to natural man, and the basic truths about man and his relationship of dependence on God can be known through the use of natural reason. What is worthy of note, even simply from the sociological point of view, is that the previously universal phenomenon of religion is decreasing in importance today. The organized threats from atheistic Communism are in most places a thing of the past, but the antireligious prejudices of Enlightenment ideology seem as virulent today as ever.

Pope John Paul II has often mentioned consumerism and secularism as constituting significant threats to modern cultures by driving out religion and dulling religious sensibilities. The pope has often spoken of the "theoretical atheism" of the East and of the "practical atheism" of the West.

Cultural attitudes that increasingly refuse to acknowledge an objective order to the world effectively result in a refusal to acknowledge the God who created it and bestowed its objectivity upon it. If there is no objective created order, judged by God to be "good," then there is no possibility of acting on behalf of an objective good. "Goods" become whatever one subjectively desires, and one's decision to obtain whatever one subjectively desires is graced today with the appellation "conscience." Properly understood, conscience is an act of the intellect judging a contemplated or performed action to be good because it conforms to the goodness of the objective moral order. As John Paul points out in *Veritatis Splendor,* "Once the idea of a universal truth about the good, knowable by human reason, is lost, inevitably the notion of conscience also changes."[37]

One time I was having dinner with a professional acquaintance who had a doctoral degree and worked in education. He went to church services every Sunday and was active in his parish. He was also an active homosexual. At dinner he said to me: "You know, we gays (homosexuals) want just what you straights (heterosexuals) want. We want someone to love. We want to have children and to raise a family." I told my acquaintance that his sentiments were very noble indeed (even as I was convinced that they would be impossible to realize). But I asked, "Don't you think that God has a plan for the way in which families are to come into being?" "Well, I used to think that," he said, "but not anymore."

That man, for all his "religious" activity was a "practical atheist," dismissing God as having any design for his creation. With no design to creation, there is no objective truth in accord with which conscience can make sound judgments about contemplated or past actions. Without God, there can be no conscience, if conscience is understood as the act of the practical intellect in accord with objective truth guiding human action.

In the preface to the German language edition of Joseph Fletcher's book *Situation Ethics,* the translator says that Fletcher has attempted to construct an ethics, "*als ob es keinen Gott gäbe,*" ("as though there were no God"). Despite Fletcher's "religious" credentials as an Anglican minister and theologian, he had to remove God from his scheme of morality in order to craft an ethic that was by his own admission pragmatic, subjectivist, and relativist.

This kind of thinking has growing cultural ramifications. Increasingly, secularist culture denies the existence of a creator God, and the implications for morality of that denial are profound. Social institutions, which play some of the most critical roles in shaping culture, are increasingly influenced by the practical atheism of secularism, which results inexorably in a radical moral relativism. For example, in the United States Supreme Court case *Planned Parenthood vs. Casey,* the justices spoke of their country's constitution as having granted citizens a broad "right to define one's own concept of existence, of meaning, of the universe and of the mystery of human life."[38]

Such language gives voice to a radical subjectivism that if actually attempted to be used as a guide for public policy, would make common life virtually impossible. The fragmentation of society would seem far advanced when the highest interpreter of the document that defines a people and its common life absurdly affords each citizen the capacity to determine what reality is. It would be impossible to forge a common life on the basis of the absolute autonomy of each individual to determine what reality is and to ascribe virtually unlimited sway to the judgment of individual private conscience.

Such thinking, expressive of many cultural presuppositions in the United States, would greatly diminish the possibility of well-formed and correct consciences among the citizenry. How could a *common* good possibly be forged with such an understanding of the human perception of reality? One thinks of the Harvard Pragmatist philosopher William James, who denied the concept of a "universe" and said we must simply acknowledge "pluriverses" corresponding to the varieties of ways in which people look at the world.

Conscience depends on a sure grasp of objective reality. As John Paul II teaches in *Veritatis Splendor*, "Conscience expresses itself in acts of 'judgment' which reflect the truth about the good, and not in arbitrary 'decisions.' The maturity and responsibility of these judgments . . . are not measured by the liberation of the conscience from objective truth . . . but, on the contrary, by an insistent search for truth and by allowing oneself to be guided by that truth in one's actions."[39] However, the greater the advances of godless secularism, the greater the skepticism that there is an objective reality which can be grasped. The result is more individualism and moral relativism, and a greater disorder to society's understanding of the nature and role of conscience.

The world derives both its being and its goodness from the creative act of God, who is Being and Goodness Itself. Josef Pieper makes the claim that Western thought (and we could say, consequently Western culture) is based upon the acceptance of the metaphysical truth that Being precedes Truth, and that Truth precedes the Good.[40] And the Being that precedes all beings is, of course, God. If there is no *Ipsum Esse*, there is no *esse* and no *essentia* to be discovered in the created order. It will be an impossible task for conscience to choose the appropriate means for an individual to reach his goal of fully actualized human existence if he does not know of what that consists.

A crisis of religion means a crisis in meaning. A crisis in meaning obviously engenders a crisis in conscience.

The atheist Jean Paul Sartre understood well the significance of the relationship between the concepts of God and of human nature. Sartre wrote, "*Il n'y a pas de nature humaine, puis qu'il n'y a pas de Dieu pour la concevoir*"[41] ("There is no human nature because there is no God to conceive of it").

The existentialism of Sartre begins from an expressly atheistic point of view and consequently denies the idea of creation. With the loss of the awareness of creation, there is the loss of meaning. All becomes absurd, meaningless. If there is any meaning to our existence, it is what man bestows on it.

Catholic philosopher Josef Pieper insists that Sartre's insight is profoundly correct in its conclusion if the first premise is correct. Of course, the premise that there is no God is false, but Pieper points out that Sartre's reasoning shows the extent to which "the doctrine of creation is the concealed but basic foundation of classical Western metaphysics."[42] Pieper argues that things have an essential nature only insofar as they are fashioned by thought. About this Sartre was correct. Man has a creative intellect and can fashion "things." For example, he can conceive of and fashion a letter opener. Therefore, we can speak of something *being* a letter opener or having the essence of a letter opener. And it is because God has conceived man, Pieper points out, that we can speak of human nature.

Pieper, of course, is an expositor of the thought of Thomas Aquinas. St. Thomas argues that all things have a nature because they have been creatively conceived by God. St. Thomas writes: "This very fact that a creature has its special and finite substance shows that it comes from a principle."[43] The Christian, and indeed even the philosopher through the use of natural reason, will know that there is an Ultimate Creative Principle and that, as a result, the world has an intelligible nature as creation and that man has an enduring nature. There is such a thing as human nature precisely—and only—because there is a Creator.

If there were no God, there would be no human nature. If there were no human nature, there would be nothing against which our intellect in the act of conscience could judge the morality of our contemplated or executed action, that is, its appropriateness for our nature achieving its fullness. Conscience is often referred to as the voice of God within us. Such an expression would indicate that men are able to perceive within themselves the plan that God had in creating them. St. Paul teaches this: "When Gentiles who do not have the law keep it as by instinct, these men although without the law serve as a law for themselves. They show that the demands of the law are written in their hearts. Their conscience bears witness together with that law, and their thoughts will accuse or defend them."[44]

Man can look to his own nature to understand what will most assuredly lead to his own fulfillment. This is because his very being is created by God and is good. As St. Thomas insists: "God 'has created all things that they might be' (Wisdom 1:14) and not that they might revert to nothingness."[45] All being is good (*Omne ens est bonum*). In seeking the good in moral action, one seeks to actualize oneself more fully. As St. Thomas teaches: "The good is that for which all things strive . . . all beings strive for their perfection."[46]

That is why it is so important to choose only true goods and not counterfeit ones, which may have great appeal but will not lead to one's being ordered in accord with reason to one's proper and ultimate end. Such judgments leading to choice would be impossible without the capacity of the conscience to judge between good and evil on the basis of truth. *Dignitatis Humanae*, the *Decree on Religious Liberty* from the Second Vatican Council, insists that one of the principal tasks of the church is "to announce and teach authentically that Truth which is Christ, and at the same time with her authority to declare and confirm the principles of the moral order which derive from human nature itself."[47] The decree makes this assertion in the paragraph that speaks to the importance of forming one's conscience in accord with the truth.

The doctrine of creation means that there is an objective, fundamentally unchanging human nature. Professor Spaemann insists on the necessity of this fact for morality. He explains: "If there were no such thing as the basic structure of human nature, whereby certain things are considered reasonable or unreasonable, then the command to love one another would be meaningless and could be replaced by whatever we wanted, for it could be filled with any content."[48]

But this, of course, is the source of the modern moral problem and of our contemporary crisis of conscience. Professor Spaemann says it is a "result of latent atheism." Of course, in Marxist-Leninism the atheism was not latent. And in our secularized societies of the world the underlying atheism of many of our cultural presuppositions is becoming increasingly less "latent." It is becoming not only explicit but increasingly militant.

The belief in the radical autonomy of the individual is a corollary of atheism; together they constitute two of the most fundamental of our cultural presuppositions today. But there is a quite legitimate fear of heteronomy. The coercive imposition of the will of another would destroy freedom and violate human dignity. Kant was right about that.

In fact, however, there is no hint of heteronomy in a morality grounded in the doctrine of creation, because the moral law is but an expression of one's very nature. Man's very being comes from an external Source—God. But there is a way in which the Source does not remain external. In the very act of creation, the image of the Source becomes an attribute of man himself, body and soul.

The pope speaks of the interior appeal to one's conscience for guidance as an "interior dialogue of man with himself." But he goes on and says that "it is also a dialogue of man with God, the author of the law, the primordial image and final end of man."[49] In arguing against an interpretation of the "fundamental option," which would leave particular actions non-constitutive of the individual in favor of a "transcendental," "athematic" choice for God, the pope insists that every freely chosen action is constitutive of man exactly because it either conforms with or deviates from man as he is and the God who created him. "[F]reedom is not only the choice for one or another particular action; it is also, within that choice, a *decision about oneself* and a setting of one's life for or against the Good, for or against the Truth, and ultimately for or against God."[50]

The pope speaks elsewhere in *Veritatis Splendor* of the intrinsic link between man acting in his own true self-interest and at the same time acting for God. "Acting is morally good when the choices of freedom are in conformity with man's true good and thus express the voluntary ordering of the person toward his ultimate end: God himself, the supreme good in whom man finds his full and perfect happiness."[51] The pope insists in this section of the encyclical that there is an "essential connection between the moral value of an act and man's final end."

The concerns of Kant about heteronomy, about a law imposed from without, and the concerns of contemporary man that his nature must be defined in terms of freedom, seem to be answered by the pope in what is fundamentally a Thomistic analysis. A succinct definition of morality by the pope gives no hint of an imposed legalism. He writes: "The rational ordering of the human act to the good in its truth and the voluntary pursuit of that good, known by reason, constitute morality. . . . Activity is morally good when it attests to and expresses the voluntary ordering of the person to his ultimate end and the conformity of a concrete action with the human good as it is acknowledged in its truth by reason."[52] Man is free, but his freedom consists in performing actions which perfect his very being as it is ordered toward ultimate bliss in its Source and End: God himself. Man is not God, but without God man is unintelligible. He is defined in terms of his origin and his end. Similarly the natural law is unintelligible without the eternal law of God, since the natural law is by definition the conscious participation of the rational creature in the eternal law.

The true nature of intrinsically evil acts is also to be understood, not in terms of the violation of an externally imposed precept, but rather in terms of a violation of one's own good. Certain actions are intrinsically evil precisely because they can never conform to the goodness of man's created, that is, given, nature. Nor can the act (which is judged to be intrinsically disordered) conform to the goodness of God, the possession of whom constitutes man's complete happiness. The pope writes: "The primary and decisive element for moral judgment is the object of the human act, which establishes whether it is *capable of being ordered to the good and to the ultimate end, which is God.*"[53] The purpose of the Ten Commandments, for example, is to safeguard basic human goods from violation and to assist everyone in finding true happiness. Intrinsically evil acts simply do no one any good, despite their occasional allure.

"Reason attests," the pope writes, "that there are objects of the human act which are by their nature 'incapable of being ordered' to God, because they radically contradict the good of the person made in his image."[54] It should be obvious from these few citations that a true rational ethic would find it impossible to speak of human goods, happiness, morality, law, or intrinsically evil acts without reference to God, who is the Supreme Good and the Source of all Truth.

All of this that has been said, however, is on the natural level. Reasonable people ought to be able to see the truth of it. Philosopher Ralph McInerny quotes St. Thomas to show the link between the natural act of conscience and its supernatural source and end. "It is clear that conscience is said to bind by the power of the divine precept."[55] In other words, it binds by virtue of its ordination to God. Msgr. Ignacio Carrasco writes that a noble and pure conscience can be seen in the "submission of the created mind to uncreated wisdom."[56]

These insights are of natural religion not of revelation. Any well-ordered society must acknowledge them and build upon them. John Henry Newman calls attention to the fact that the wicked "naturally" feel guilt and at times terror, by which they implicitly acknowledge the "supernatural" reality of God as the source of the moral law. He also sees in such sentiments evidence of the inescapable link between religion and morality.

> "The wicked flees, when no one pursueth"; then why does he flee? whence his terror? Who is it that he sees in solitude, in darkness, in the hidden chambers of his heart? If the cause of these emotions does not belong to this visible world, the Object to which his perception is directed must be Supernatural and Divine; and thus the phenomena of Conscience, as a dictate, avail to impress the imagination with the picture of a Supreme Governor, a Judge, holy, just, powerful, all-seeing, retributive, and is the creative principle of religion, as the Moral Sense is the principle of ethics.[57]

But, of course, the insights and truths granted through revelation do not contradict what is known through natural reason. What God has done for mankind in Jesus Christ effects a reconciliation between fallen man and his true Good that never could be fully possessed without God's grace. True freedom finally becomes a possibility for man because he has been set free from sin, has had his ignorance with regard to what is truly good for him expelled, has been empowered by grace to live the supernatural life to which he has been called, and has been filled with a love for the true Good that far transcends his own natural capabilities. As Father Giertych puts it, God, through grace, "liberates goodness in man" and now mysteriously manifests himself to the world "in sanctified human activity."[58]

The Restoration of Conscience and Culture

In both *Veritatis Splendor* and *Evangelium Vitae* the pope quotes Romans 12:2: "Do not conform yourselves to this age but be transformed by the renewal of your mind, so that you may judge what is God's will, what is good, pleasing and perfect."

The challenge to God's goodness and to the good of humanity posed by modernity will most likely increase. As the Orvieto Conference, which engendered these papers, was taking place, Pope John Paul II had taken on the inhuman policies of modernity as they were being articulated by those powerful nations and interests that had given shape to the United Nations Conference on Development and Population, which took place in Cairo in September 1994. The pope personally wrote to the heads of states of all member countries of the United Nations to plead for protection for the unborn and for women facing troubled pregnancies, who were profoundly threatened by the program prepared for the conference, which would later influence U.N. policies. While the Catholic scholars were gathered in Italy in May of 1994 for the conference that gave rise to this book, they learned of the depths of the pope's concerns about the Cairo Conference. They heard that he had asked all Catholics to begin praying daily the prayer to St. Michael the Archangel in anticipation of the Conference and the struggle between good and evil that would take place there.

Many consider the pope's interventions with heads of states and through the Vatican delegation to have changed the direction and tone of the entire United Nations Conference.

Clearly the subject matter for conscience does not remain abstract. Morality and conscience are about concrete human decisions and actions. But the cultural odds against a sound understanding of morality and conscience in our own day seem utterly insuperable. The situation sometimes looks hopeless. What does the Catholic do?

Msgr. Carlo Caffarra, now Archbishop of Ferrara-Comacchio, was keenly aware of the dilemma facing the Catholic today when he addressed the Orvieto Conference. The Catholic is faced with, as he puts it, the impossible possibility and the possible impossibility. He sees humanity standing at the shore of the Red Sea with Pharaoh's army and certain destruction behind and, at the same time, the waters of the Red Sea and certain death ahead. In the face of such a situation what does the person of faith and hope do? He advances.

As Christians, there are a multitude of ways in which culture can be restored and conscience renewed, but none of them without a price. The first thing, of course, is to live faithfully in accord with one's own conscience shaped by the truth of Catholic teaching. In private and social life, in personal witness, in professional activities, in scholarly writing, the truth about conscience and man's relation to God must be put forth at every opportunity.

Morality is a concrete, practical science. Conscience guides us in concrete, specific actions in unique circumstances. Therefore, the most critical thing for the person of faith to do is to cling to and to bear witness to true humanity as it is enfleshed, embodied, concretized, historicized, particularized in Jesus Christ, body and soul, humanity and divinity.

In the second section of *Veritatis Splendor* the pope subjects contemporary erroneous moral theories to rigorous philosophical analysis and critique. Having shown their deficiencies through careful scholarly scrutiny, the pope nonetheless does not attach ultimate hope to such scholarship. In the third part of *Veritatis Splendor* the pope says that the real hope for the transformation of the world does not rest with the church's considerable scholarly tradition. The church, the pope tells us, finds

> the "secret" of its educative power . . . not so much in doctrinal statements . . . as in *constantly looking to the Lord Jesus*. Each day the Church looks to Christ with unfailing love, fully aware that the true and final answer to the problem of morality lies in him alone. In a particular way, it is in the Crucified Christ that the Church finds the answer to the question troubling so many people today: how can obedience to universal and unchanging moral norms respect the uniqueness and individuality of the person, and not represent a threat to his freedom and dignity?[59]

Christ Crucified shows us that there is no contradiction between living in conformity with unchanging norms and exercising our freedom, which is the mark of human dignity. The dignity of conscience derives from its conformity to the truth, and it is only the true that is good.

St. Thomas asks in the *Summa Theologica* how the passion of Christ could have been virtuous and meritorious, since virtue implies action, and passion (*passio*) implies passivity and being acted upon. St. Thomas concedes that our Lord was indeed passive and acted upon in his body during the time of his betrayal and crucifixion. But he goes on to point out that Christ was intensely *active* in his sufferings because he inwardly clung tenaciously and faithfully to the Good.[60]

Likewise, Christians must cling steadfastly to the Good as they are faced with impossible situations, as was Moses at the shore of the Red Sea and our Lord was on Calvary. The moral life, the pope insists, "is not a matter only of disposing oneself to hear a teaching and obediently accepting a commandment. More radically, it involves *holding fast to the very person of Jesus.*"[61] And, above all, it means holding fast to Jesus, perfect man, as he hangs on the cross, refusing to relinquish his hold on the Good, the only source of human happiness and fulfillment.

There is reason for hope, even in our day, because human beings are so constituted that the voice of conscience can almost always be reawakened within them, even when they have fallen into depraved practices. It is always "the good" that remains the key to the moral thought of John Paul II–even when evil is chosen. "If man does evil," writes John Paul II, "the just judgment of his conscience remains within him as a witness to the universal truth of the good, as well as to the malice of his particular choice. But the verdict of conscience remains in him also a pledge of hope and mercy."[62]

In *Evangelium Vitae* the pope points out that it is the judgment of conscience that leads those who perpetrate the wicked deeds of abortion or euthanasia to use euphemisms to mislead others as to the nature of what they are doing as well as to attempt to quiet the voice of their own conscience. Therefore, he tells us that it is most salutary to use clear and explicit language in dealing with those acts that pose a threat to innocent human life. In such a way, through a firm statement of the truth, we can hope to reawaken conscience. As St. Augustine tells us: "There is no soul, however perverse, but which can in some way still reason, in whose conscience God does not speak."[63] If one can still make use of his reason, there is hope that his conscience, which is after all an act of reason, can be rectified.

The pope insists that the relationship between man's freedom (to which modern man lays uncompromising claim) and God's law has its center in "the moral conscience, [which] is manifested and realized in human acts. It is precisely through his acts that man attains perfection as man, as one who is called to seek his Creator of his own accord and freely to arrive at full and blessed perfection by cleaving to him."[64]

The Holy Father concludes both *Veritatis Splendor* and *Evangelium Vitae* with an invocation of the Blessed Mother. He surely does so because she was the freest and happiest and most fulfilled of all God's creatures, because she so lovingly surrendered herself to the good and clung to it resolutely even when "the sword pierced her own heart." The victory against evil has indeed already been won in Christ. That victory will become each of ours, however, as we embrace the cross with him, and then through our transformation in Christ, culture itself will be transformed. Those must indeed be assured of triumph who have such a powerful heavenly intercessor as we have in the Mother of God. There are many confessors and martyrs who with their Queen provide us today with encouraging examples of victory by their having been attentive to the guidance of their conscience as it enabled them to cling unflinchingly to goodness and to truth.

Notes

1. *Evangelium Vitae* (hereafter EV), 25 March 1995, 4.
2. *Veritatis Splendor* (hereafter VS), 6 August 1993, 93.
3. John Henry Newman, *An Essay in Aid of a Grammar of Assent* (Notre Dame, Indiana: University of Notre Dame Press, 1979) (1870), p. 98.
4. *Dominum et Vivificantem*, 18 May 1986, 43.
5. VS, 60.
6. Cresacre More, *The Life of Sir Thomas More, Knight* (Athens, Pennsylvania: Riverside Press, 1941) (London: 1726), p. 179.
7. EV, 21.
8. Karol Wojtyla, *Sign of Contradiction* (New York: The Seabury Press, 1979), p. 140.

9. Paul Johnson, *Pope John Paul II and the Restoration of the Catholic Church* (New York: St. Martin's Press, 1981), p. 81.

10. Apostolic Exhortation *Reconciliatio et Poenitentia,* 2 December 1984, 18. The questions contained in the quotation are from the *Angelus* address of the Holy Father on 14 March 1982.

11. EV, 64.

12. EV, 14.

13. EV, 17.

14. EV, 17.

15. EV, 18.

16. EV, 20.

17. EV, 24.

18. EV, 11.

19. VS, 4.

20. James Russell Lowell, "The Present Crisis," 1844. Cf. *The Hymnal 1940 Companion* (New York: The Church Pension Fund, 1949), pp. 312, 489, and *The Hymnal 1940* (New York: The Church Pension Fund, 1940), p. 519.

21. In my own education, I had read all of those authors before I was ever introduced to the writings of St. Thomas Aquinas.

22. Pope John Paul II, *Crossing the Threshold of Hope* (New York: Random House, 1994).

23. *Kant's Critique of Practical Reason and Other Works on the Theory of Ethics,* 6th ed., trans. T. K. Abott (London, 1909) p. 191.

24. Immanuel Kant, *Grundlegung zur Metaphysik der Sitten,* C4, p. 265. "*Selbst der Heilige der Evangelii muss zuvor mit unserem Ideal der sittlichen Vollkommenheit verglichen werden, ehe man dafür erkennt.*"

25. Richard Kroner, *Von Kant bis Hegel* (Tübingen, 1921), vol. I, p. 153. Quoted by Josef Pieper in *Reality and the Good* (Chicago: Henry Regnery and Company, 1967), p. 48.

26. EV, 35.

27. EV, 33.

28. Martin Luther, *Commentary on Galatians* in *Martin Luther: Selections from His Writings,* ed. John Dillenberger (Garden City, New York: Anchor Books, 1961), p. 131.

29. "For if the blood of goats and bulls and the sprinkling of a heifer's ashes can sanctify those who are defiled so that their flesh is cleansed, how much more will the blood of Christ, who through the eternal spirit offered himself unblemished to God, cleanse our consciences from dead works to worship the living God" (Hebrews 9:13,14, *New American Bible*).

30. Cf. Roland Bainton, *Here I Stand: Martin Luther* (New York: Mentor Book, 1955), p. 175.

31. *Westminster Confession,* I, v.

32. John Calvin, *Institutes of Religion,* 1.7.5.

33. Gustavo Gutiérrez, *A Theology of Liberation* (Maryknoll, New York: Orbis Books, 1973), p. 268.

34. Ibid., p. 274.

35. *Instruction on Certain Aspects of the "Theology of Liberation,"* Rome, 6 August 1984; *Instruction on Christian Freedom and Liberation*, Rome, 22 March 1986.

36. EV, 20.

37. VS, 32.

38. 112 S. Ct. 2791, 2807

39. VS, 61

40. Joseph Pieper, *Prudence* (New York: Pantheon Books, 1959), p. 14. Cf. *Summa Theologica*, IIaIIae, 47, 5 ad 3.

41. Jean-Paul Sartre, *L'existentialisme est un humanisme* (Paris: Nagel, 1946), p. 22.

42. Josef Pieper, *The Silence of St. Thomas* (Chicago: Henry Regnery and Company, 1965), p. 58.

43. *Summa Theologica*, Ia, 93, 6.

44. Romans 2:14-16.

45. *Quaestiones Quodlibetales* 4, 4.

46. *Summa Theologica*, Ia, 5, 1.

47. *Dignitatis Humanae*, 14.

48. Page 127 below.

49. VS, 58.

50. VS, 65.

51. VS, 72.

52. Ibid., 72.

53. Ibid., 79.

54. Ibid., 80.

55. *In II Sent.*, dist. 39, q. 3, a.1, ad 3.

56. Page 148 below.

57. Newman, *Grammar*, p. 101.

58. Page 56 below.

59. VS, 85.

60. Cf. *Summa Theologica* 2a2ae, q. 123, art. 6 ad 2. "*Dicendum quod sustinere importat quidem passionem corporis, sed actum animae fortissime inhaerentis bono, ex quo sequitur quod non cedat passioni corporali iam imminenti. Virtus autem magis attenditur circa animam quam circa corpus.*"

61. VS, 19.

62. Ibid., 61.

63. *De Sermone Domini in Monte*, 2, cap. 9, 32.

64. Ibid., 71.

3

Conscience and the Liberum Arbitrium

WOJCIECH GIERTYCH, O.P.

Introduction

The American convert Richard Neuhaus, commenting on the papal encyclical *Centesimus Annus*, noted in 1992:

> When Vatican II confirmed the *Declaration on Religious Liberty*,
> many felt that the authoritative Church, finally but unwillingly,
> came to terms with the modern world. Twenty-five years later it is
> clear that the Catholic Church, the oldest and the most universal
> institution in the world, is the most serious champion of human
> liberty.[1]

The church is not afraid of human liberty, even though liberty is
the main motto of dissenting theologians who attempt to defend the
arbitrary orientation of a conscience that dares to ignore truth. The
citation of Richard Neuhaus refers to the role the church and the present
pontificate have played in the struggle for an essentially spiritual and,
consequently, economic and political freedom in the world and, in
particular, in Eastern Europe. The focus of the church, however, is
not limited to freedom from external repression. It is primarily directed at that inner spiritual liberty of the Christian who is led by the
Holy Spirit.

The purpose of this essay is to study the nature of spiritual freedom and its relationship to conscience in light of the teachings of St. Thomas Aquinas. The main thrust of the objections raised today against the moral teaching of the church lies in the desire to interpret freedom in such a manner that moral choices made in the name of conscience could be indifferent to the requirements of objective truth. The defense of the rooting of conscience in objective truth should not, however, blur the creative aspect of reason. Man must make moral decisions in the hubbub of concrete practical situations that affront him. Decisions in which conscience is active, if they consequently lead to demanding acts of virtue, are creative. The specific character of Christian living lies in the undertaking of acts of virtue in which supernatural charity is operative. For the gift of self that these acts imply to be true, they have to be free, that is, to spring from a mature and independent personality capable of discerning a need in a novel and responsible manner. The creative aspect of human decision-making should not therefore disappear in a reflection on the nature of conscience. It is true that conscience cannot be creative as far as the norm is concerned. A conscience that would see itself entitled to create moral norms for itself would necessarily fall into the trap of blind subjectivity, incapable of leaning on any solid foundation, lost in a nihilist vacuum, with only the fleeting whims of social expectations and personal psychic experiences to lean on. Conscience, therefore, cannot demand creative freedom for itself with respect to norms. It must, however, be creative with respect to the act it impels and with respect to the act it judges after its execution.

The capacity of conscience to generate good acts is by no means simple and obvious. For it to develop, it requires spiritual freedom and a transformation of the faculties. The main function of interior liberty consists in the consistent and responsible choice of that which is objectively good, that is, in choosing that which is in accord with the nature of things. Or rather, it should be said that the consistent and responsible choice of objective good generates an inner liberty. The capacity to choose and to choose well, however, can be seriously distorted. I can say from my pastoral experience in Poland that the spiritual ruin brought about by Communism in many people has caused, among other things, not only an inability to recognize what is true and good, which is a deformation of conscience, but also the inability to transform the judgment of conscience into an act. Often the apprehension of true values among people who are hungry for God is speedy and accompanied by an authentic fascination, but what is lacking is the capacity to translate it from the judgment of conscience into a stable and consistent choice. The education of conscience must envisage not only the capacity to discern truth, but also the capacity to transform discernment into action. One of the reasons the judgment of conscience is often eschewed is that it is demanding and requires spiritual vigor. The humiliating inability to persevere in the choice that is recognized as good leads often, then, to the espousal of theories that deny that good or claim that the recognition of objective truth is impossible. The replacement of the standard of truth by subjective personal whims derives from the recognition of moral weakness that is not accompanied by faith in divine succor. Due to the lack of humble surrender to the living God, the step then is very easy toward a rationalization that endeavors to escape from the requirements of truth as it has been presented by conscience.

The development of spiritual maturity based on a humble acceptance of the need of divine aid leads to an inner liberty that permits perseverant choices. Liberty is a profound value but it is not a value in itself. It denotes the capacity to choose value, and to choose correctly, that is, in accord with the objective structure of human nature and its finality. A reflection on the nature of conscience and on its mode of functioning, therefore, should neither fear freedom nor give the impression of fearing it. Freedom is a great gift, promised by Jesus and awaited with impatience by the church. It is not without reason that the church sings *Veni ad liberandum nos!* The moral teaching of the church, therefore, should assume the desire for freedom, illuminating its nature and explaining the laws of the development of spiritual freedom.

It is my impression that the encyclical *Veritatis Splendor* (without denying its obvious value!) could do with a paragraph on the dynamics of interior freedom that would balance the chapter on conscience. The perspective of a mature and well-functioning conscience in a personality that enjoys the freedom of the children of God and a presentation of the means and ways of attaining that spiritual liberty are needed in a comprehensive synthesis of moral theology. In this essay I will strive to describe the nature of spiritual liberty and the function exercised by conscience in good creative action. It is the quality of the decision that is entailed in creative action and its concomitance with the intrinsic movements of reason and will as well as with the movement of the Holy Spirit that supplies to the decision the characteristic of supreme liberty.

The Nature and Function of Moral Theology

In this reflection upon the nature and role of conscience within spiritual liberty, I believe it is necessary to place the object of our research within a theological context. The point of departure in ethical reflection conditions the understanding and the placement of a topic within a wider general picture. If the moral teaching of the church is often rejected, the refusal is sometimes caused by a misunderstanding of the place of Christian morals within the hierarchy of truths. The organizing center of Christian moral teaching should be as close as possible to the revealed paschal mystery of God, who gives himself to men for their salvation in Jesus Christ. A moral theology that is centered on the moral law, which prescribes those acts that are to be executed and those that are to be omitted, and on conscience, which is to apply these precepts, is certainly legitimate, but it is grossly impoverished. The way in which moral theology is tackled and presented in the church conditions the reactions that it elicits.

The nature and scope of moral theology has to be clearly defined before the particular question of conscience and freedom can be discussed theologically. The encyclical *Veritatis Splendor* defines moral theology as:

> a reflection concerned with "morality," with the good and evil of human acts and of the person who performs them. . . . It is also "theology," inasmuch as it acknowledges that the origin and end of moral action are found in the One who "alone is good" and who, by giving himself to man in Christ, offers him the happiness of divine life.[2]

In this definition of moral theology, the focus is above all on morality, that is, on

the rational ordering of the human act to the good in its truth and
the voluntary pursuit of that good, known by reason.[3]

The object of attention in this science is the moral fact of acts, a fact
that also can be the object of attention of other disciplines, such as
philosophical ethics, sociology, and psychology. What gives to this
discipline a theological dimension is the source and the end of the act,
that is, its reference to God–a reference that is perceived also by moral
philosophy–and the fact that man is endowed by God with beatitude.
If I understand this definition correctly, it proposes that in moral theology attention should be focused on morality, taking into account
the extra stream of light that is thrown upon it by revelation, a stream
that brings order to the observed object and clarifies pressing questions but always remains an extra light flowing from without. I would
define such a discipline not as moral theology but rather as theological ethics. It deals not with God but with morality, that is, with human
activity, which either pursues the good presented by the objective
norm or pursues the evil, in which reference to the norm is absent.
The relationship between the act and the good can be analyzed by
independent reason. The addition of the perspective of faith supple-
ments the analysis with a discernment of the openness to grace in the
acting subject and with a strengthening of the authority of the norm,
because it is based upon revelation. The direction of moral activity is
enriched because God is shown as the end by revelation. The center
of attention, however, remains the moral fact, which can, of course,
be the object of study without the perspective of faith.

I am convinced that fruitful moral teaching of the church requires a
different perspective for moral theology, a perspective I believe is to
be found in a theological reading of the work of Aquinas. Moral theology is a theology, and theology is a science about God. It has God
as he has revealed himself as the main object of its study. Theology is
based upon revelation, in which we receive in faith the mystery that
God himself has revealed primarily about himself, and, with the aid
of reason enlightened by faith, we attempt to penetrate this mystery
and present it to the student so as to awaken in him a deeper faith, a
faith that opens unto the salvific power of God. At the same time, we
discern a basic concordance of the data of revelation with the sincere

discoveries of reason. Since God is the object of study in theology, what distinguishes moral theology from other parts of theology is the specific mode of the presence of God. There are three modes of the presence of God to which the three parts of the *Summa Theologica* of St. Thomas correspond. First of all, God is omnipresent as the Lord and Creator. Second, he is present in a different manner through grace within souls and within the moral activity of believers. And, third, God is present in Christ, in the hypostatic union and in the sacraments.

Moral theology deals, therefore, with God present by grace in human activity. The attention in moral theology is focused not on morality as such, but on God, who manifests himself mysteriously in sanctified human activity. Such an approach necessarily views the summit of the spiritual journey of man. It perceives in the light of faith the *imago Dei*, present in mature, creative, and loving human activity liberated by the Holy Spirit. Moral theology depicts how the integrative, deifying, and, at the same time, beatifying presence of God manifests itself in the human psyche, in action, in free choices, in the responding to values in moral acts. This dynamic action of God within human freedom finds a stable direction in the supernatural habits that stimulate good actions, that is, in the infused virtues and gifts of the Holy Spirit. Furthermore, God directs toward the good also from without, by making values explicit through moral law, both natural and revealed. Particular moral theology that continues the search for God, centers upon the fecundity of the divine presence as it manifests itself in faith that is operative in divine love. Charity elicits in various aspects of human life the whole panorama of virtues. In various states and vocations it manifests itself in a variegated manner but is always the fruit of that same sanctifying and hidden yet dynamically stimulating presence of God.

Moral theology deals, therefore, not just with norms or with good and sinful acts, but with God, who, through grace, liberates goodness in man. If the norm is mentioned, then it is as a signpost, a helping direction that ultimately consists in the law of the Spirit, in which the grace of the Holy Spirit becomes a direct norm of activity of the spiritually transformed person.

With this theological perspective in mind, open to the mystery of divine presence within moral activity, the study of the nature and function of conscience and its relationship to spiritual liberty can be undertaken. Attention to the divine hand that activates the conscience in its mobilizing function, of course, conditions the study of reason and will in their functioning. Theological questions sharpen the philosophical mind. Conscience and liberty can be studied with a purely rational frame of mind, but the theological question helps to formulate the problem and corrects an errant avenue of research. The aim of theology, which is the entry into the revealed mystery, conditions the choice of philosophical categories that are used. Not every philosophical system is capable of illuminating the mystery that is being studied. That is why the choice of the system has to be dictated by the requirements of the truth that is studied rather than by the social acceptability of the philosophical terminology used.

The Liberum Arbitrium *as an Expression of Liberty in the Holy Spirit*

St. Thomas Aquinas in his prologue to the *IIa pars*, which announces the general perspective of the moral section of the *Summa*, defines with the help of a quotation from St. John Damascene the divine image in man as comprising three specific elements: the intellectual nature, the *liberum arbitrium*, and the fact that man has the source of his management within himself. In the search for the divine image in man, therefore, the moral section of theology studies in what particular way man is a principle of his own acts, acting out of his *liberum arbitrium* and his own self-domination.[4] The divine image in the acting person is fully legible only to the extent that the entire personality is divinized through grace from within, that is, at the end of a long process of spiritual growth. Nevertheless, a glimpse of the divine presence can be perceived in sanctified human activity insofar as that good activity flows from the *liberum arbitrium* and is expressive of a personal and mature management of one's affairs. The *liberum arbitrium*, that is, the capacity to make mature, free, and good choices, acquires therefore in the mind of Aquinas an outstanding significance as the visible mark of divine presence.

The nature of the *liberum arbitrium* and the function of conscience within it, as well as the ways in which the capacity for free choice may be repressed, therefore, are to be studied so that the perspective of spiritual liberation may be presented. A true appraisal of spiritual liberty is the best response we can give to theories of conscience that ascribe to it the right to create its own norms. The desire for creativity in moral action is a true desire that is not to be denied. Moral teaching will best fulfill its role when it depicts the nature and scope of spiritual liberty brought out by the power of the Holy Spirit, and when it presents the ways and means of developing that creative liberty.

The Liberum Arbitrium *as a Fruit of Both Reason and the Will*

Aquinas's favorite term for describing liberty is the expression *liberum arbitrium*. This should not be translated "free will" but "free choice." Liberty consists in the capacity to make good and responsible choices. An act is fully human when it is the expression of a free choice, that is, of a choice in which all the spiritual faculties are involved in a mature manner. Liberty requires the engagement of reason, that is, of conscience, which conditions the willing of the will.

According to Aquinas, the *liberum arbitrium* is the result of the mutual cooperation of both reason and will, in which the two faculties are dependent upon one another.[5] The judgment of a truly free choice is undertaken by reason, which supplies the ground for the choice, and so the core of liberty lies in the judgment of reason, which influences the choice.[6] Whereas what makes the choice free in the *liberum arbitrium* is the will. It is the act of the will that causes the judgment of reason in free choice to be free.[7] The will moves reason, urging it to pass a judgment, and reason, in turn, moves the will by proposing an appropriate object. It could be said, therefore, that the two faculties influence one another in a dialectical manner.[8]

The free choice is therefore the consequence of the mutual action of both spiritual faculties. It is not antecedent to the judgment of reason and the movement of the will. The dignity of man, who is an image of God, lies not only in the fact that he undertakes action, but also in the fact that he discerns the end of his action; he discerns the appropriate means and also their ordination toward the end. All this is undertaken by reason, which passes judgment and decides about what is presented to the will as an object of the will's willing.[9] The act of free choice can then be defined as willing directed by the judgment of reason. It is simultaneously rational and volitional.

For a clearer understanding of spiritual liberty and of the role that conscience plays in the generation of free acts, the nature and mutual dependence of reason and will need to be studied.

The Nature of Conscience

Conscience traditionally is defined as the act of practical reason. Just as theoretical reason is endowed with the first principles of reasoning, which grant a logical foundation to all intellectual reflection, so practical reason is endowed with the first principle of action, known as *synderesis*, which, in an innate and infallible judgment, assesses that good is to be done and that evil is to be avoided. This primary judgment of the practical reason is the source and foundation of the judgments of conscience. Practical reason begins with the spark of *synderesis*, and, using the light it receives from the instinctively known moral law and from its own experience and education, and taking into account the unique circumstances with which it is affronted, it issues a judgment concerning the act to be executed or passes a judgment on the act that took place.

It is clear, therefore, that reason has to be exercised so that it can truly, without failing, perceive what is objectively true and good. The human intellect is created as endowed with an attraction toward truth. This natural desire for truth is the source of contemplation in man, the source of all sciences. Man is not capable of knowing the entire truth. It requires effort and training to perceive what is true. But truth is a spontaneous object of concern for the intellect. Furthermore, the intellect moved by love has the fascinating capacity to transcend itself and to open toward mysteries that exceed the limits of reason so as to receive them in faith—out of love for the Giver of these revealed truths. The formation of conscience, which presents values and teaches reason to discern them, has an obvious ally in the natural inclination of the intellect for truth. Man is instinctively drawn to what is true.

The capacity of the intellect to discern truth, its intuitive attraction to it, as well as the capacity of reason to reflect upon the inherent logic and consistency of perceived truth can be developed. The primary concern of education, therefore, should be to develop the contemplative mind so that it can repose in truth, in truth that elicits satisfaction. It is only when a particular truth has been perceived by the contemplative mind that it conditions practical reason to issue a judgment.

Since the intellect has an inherent capacity to perceive truth, it is the truth of reality that binds the conscience. Moral law points out that reality without denying the cognitive capacities of the mind. The function of moral law is to enlighten the mind so that the conscience can issue an appropriate judgment. Both natural law and the summit of the revealed law are unwritten; they function as interior instincts that enlighten the reason, presenting the insights of common sense and the direct suggestions of the Holy Spirit. The education of conscience avails itself of written moral exhortations that are the fruit of both rational reflection and divine revelation, but their primary aim is to awaken the perception of our interior instincts.

Conscience belongs to the order of cognition and not to the order of appetition. The rational structure of conscience, which is an application of knowledge *con-scientia* to the moral act, brings us to distinguish carefully between the judgment of conscience, which belongs to the order of cognition, and the feeling of satisfaction or of guilt, which belongs to the order of sensitive appetition. The judgment of conscience is always rational and not emotional, although the concomitance of the rational and carnal parts of the human composite, elicits–in a healthy personality–an emotional feeling of contentment when the judgment of the conscience is followed and an emotional feeling of guilt when the judgment of conscience is not followed. This secondary emotional feeling contributes to the healthy functioning of the conscience. It does not, however, belong to its essence. It is possible that the judgment of conscience may be correct and binding for moral action, even though the complementary feeling of contentment or guilt may be minute, nonexistent, or excessive and ill-directed. In a psychopathic personality there is a constitutional rift between the judgment of reason and the emotions. A psychopath may know that his action is unreasonable, that it is contrary to the moral norm, but, due to a pathological handicap, he does not feel guilty. His emotions do not correspond to the judgment of reason. In a neurotic personality the emotions are constitutionally sound, but, due to a faulty education, their functioning is ill-directed. The emotional disturbance causes the judgment of reason, that is, of conscience, even though it may be correct, to be impeded in the practical direction of some of the emotions.

The education of conscience, therefore, should include an appropriate adjustment of the rational and emotional parts of man, so that the clear verdict of reason can be recognized and condition the will to make free choices.

The Nature of the Will

According to Aquinas, the will is a spiritual appetitive faculty distinct from the emotions. The movement of the will is not carnal; it flows from the will itself, which is spiritual. The will naturally strives to remain in the good that has been proposed to it by reason. The good that is presented to the will by reason draws out of the will a spontaneous movement toward that good.[10] In other words, there is in the will a natural attraction given to it by the Creator toward that which is good.[11] The approach of Aquinas toward the will is more optimistic than that of the modern mind, which, after Kant, sees in the will primarily an energy that inclines toward the execution of duty. The will is not a form of pressure exerted on others and oneself and on one's senses to force them into the execution of an external command. The will is above all a faculty that expresses the love and desire for the good, that is, a spontaneous drive toward the good. Any pressure toward other faculties and objects is consequent with respect to this primary drive toward the good. The will is not basically a power of coercion; rather, it is a faculty that suffers impression, that is, the stamp of the good presented by reason that elicits in the will its drive.

The natural inclination of the will instinctively moves to that which corresponds to human nature. This includes the final end of man, which is the beatifying vision of God, the cognition of truth, the preservation of being and life, and everything else that belongs to human faculties as their appropriate object.[12] Everything that can be included in the universal good is naturally willed.[13] Concrete sensitive goods elicit a sensitive appetition, that is, a movement of the emotions. But when reason discerns in them a participation in the universal good, then the will is inclined to them under the aspect of the universal good. Particular goods are incapable of necessarily attracting the will, because without them man can be happy.[14] Only the final good, that is, happiness itself, and only it, can draw out of the will an attraction without any preceding reasoning. This attraction of the will for the final end that is without any judgment of the cognitive faculties, is supremely free, because the will rejoices with a natural fulfillment of itself when it attains its appropriate object.[15] Paradoxically, therefore, the greatest liberty takes place with the determinism of the final end. The will is then most free when there is no deliberation and choice, because the will is moved by its natural inclination to that which is its final end. It is only in this context that Aquinas uses the term "free will"–*libera voluntas*–which, in modern usage, denotes an arbitrary indetermination of the will. For Aquinas, the will is most free when it is most itself; that is, when it is determined from within, according to its innate inclination toward its objective end.

That man can reject the source of true happiness that is natural for the will is interpreted by Aquinas as a symptom of the weakness of human freedom rather than as a symptom of its greatness. The angels, who cannot sin any more, enjoy a greater freedom than humans exactly because they are incapable of choosing evil. Their will is spontaneously directed toward God, and for their will, this is a sign of self-fulfillment–and therefore freedom.[16] Their will is confirmed in goodness by grace. The natural attraction to the universal good present in every creature is not strong enough to assure an eternal confirmation of the will in goodness. That is why grace is required for an enhancement of the adherence of the will to the good and therefore for an enhancement of its freedom.[17]

When the will of man is drawn to evil, it is always because some evil has appeared to it as an apparent good.[18] The will sometimes permits that it be drawn by some other particular good, proposed by the senses, and then it ignores the universal good that has been presented more or less explicitly by reason.[19] In falling into this trap, the will becomes less free.

The will, therefore, in order to defend itself from becoming less free, needs the support of reason. The undertaking of acts of free choice by both reason and will enhances the interior liberty. For the development of human maturity, it is necessary that choices be made, choices that flow from within, from a personal discovery of value by reason, and from a decision about it, and not uniquely out of obedience to an external norm. The education of conscience has to lead to the capacity for personal choices; it must therefore envisage a field of personal initiatives and also a field of personal failure.

The Role of Conscience in the Liberum Arbitrium

The act of reason has a double function in the process of executing a free and creative act because in action there are two stages of judgment. The first stage of judgment, which is strictly the stage of conscience, consists of the simple cognition of truth concerning action. That judgment is next followed by the second judgment of the *liberum arbitrium*, that is, of the mutual action of both reason and will in which the cognition supplied by the conscience is applied to the act. These two stages have to be distinguished, because the judgment of conscience may be correct, whereas the judgment of the *liberum arbitrium* may be perverted. When the judgment of conscience is made, practical reason undertakes a speculative procedure, beginning with the principles, and applies them to the contingent act that is to be carried out. But the inadequacy of the will, the attractive force of the senses, or mere laziness may cause the act perceived correctly by conscience never to be undertaken, or even its opposite chosen. The person then does not err in conscience but errs in the election of the act.[20] The judgment of conscience, therefore, is different from the judgment of choice, but it nevertheless conditions that choice. In what way does the practical reason *speculando per principia* supply the material for the choice, and how can this movement of reason ensure that the free choice is true?

Practical reason is not a faculty distinct from speculative reason. It is the same reason that becomes practical when it is directed not uniquely to pure cognition but to the act that is to be carried out. It is in view of the act that is to be executed that reason is practical, but it functions in a speculative mode supplying from the principles the necessary information for the act. The difference between the action of speculative and practical reason lies in the nature of the truth to which reason is drawn. Speculative reason as it deals with necessary beings finds its truth in the conformity of reason with the reality of being. Practical reason deals with contingent beings that may or may not exist. It cannot, therefore, find its truth in the reality of beings not yet existent. The truth of practical reason in its reflection drawn from the principles lies, therefore, as Aquinas explains, in the conformity of practical reason with the rectified appetite.[21] This explanation may seem to suggest a vicious circle. The truth of practical reason lies in its conformity with the rectified appetite, whereas the appetite is rectified by its conformity with reason. Aquinas finds the answer to this dilemma by pointing out what was said above, that the will is determined to its end by its nature. Either it moves toward that end or it moves toward other ends that are means of attaining the ultimate end. The will therefore finds its appropriate direction in its appetition of that to which it is geared by nature, whereas when the will wills a means toward that end, it is determined by reason inasmuch as it is directed to its appropriate end.[22] Practical reason, therefore, in its issuing of a judgment in free choice takes into account the natural inclination of the will toward its appropriate good, and that natural inclination, which finds its external expression in the natural law, is the guarantee of truth in the judgment of free choice. When the judgment of practical reason is applied to the act of free choice, it transposes the recognition of the inherent drive of the will to the good, as it is perceived by reason in its speculative research to that contingent act about to be made, granting it an inherent truth. The conformity of the act with the rectified will is dependent on the conformity of reason with reality in its discernment of the objective goods that attract the will. Conscience, therefore, does not create its truth in the process of issuing a free act. In the joint action of practical reason and the will in free choice, it is the act that is created, but its quality is measured by the inclination of the will to true goods as they have been objectively perceived by speculative reason. Reason and will in accord with their inherent natures are therefore creative in the act of free choice, without denying the truth of objective reality as it is presented by the moral norm and perceived by reason.

It is therefore possible to defend the creativity of the *liberum arbitrium* in its generation of acts, retaining at the same time the objectivity of moral standards, since reason and will are only truly free in their mutual action when they comply with the inherent attractiveness of that which is true and good. The education of conscience, therefore, requires the development of its capacity to perceive truly and its capacity to transpose the perceived insights into judgments of free choice.

The Development of Creativeness

Choice is fully human and fully free when all the intellectual faculties fulfill their natural role. Whenever reason refrains from directing free choice and permits that choices be made not on the basis of the judgment of conscience but, for example, on the basis of feelings, such as concupiscence, or fear, or the blind sense of obligation in response to the demands of a voluntaristic power that is perceived to be entitled to be irrational, or, even worse, when no choices are made at all and the person refrains from an action that, though not in any way obligatory, could have been undertaken, the person is in some way unfree. The will needs liberation, and reason needs enlightenment to be empowered to issue acts of free choice.

It is clear, in light of the role attributed by Aquinas to the *liberum arbitrium*, that acts which flow from a supremely free choice, that correspond to the natural inclinations of reason and will, and "create" nonexisting, contingent goods, irrespective of whether they were commanded or not, are significant in that they manifest the personal richness of the acting person. Human acts that are free, neither directly commanded by precepts nor forbidden by them but flowing from a personal conviction and decision moved by the recognition of value, certainly interest us far more than those acts that flow uniquely from obedience to commandments. It seems that they interest God more, too. Hopefully, such free acts are more numerous than those to which the precepts of the commandments directly pertain. It is the good acts undertaken freely out of a personal decision that best manifest the quality of a person.

Therefore, for Aquinas, freedom is not a given fact. It is a program of development. When free choice is exercised–when values are truly recognized by conscience, and even though they are demanding, they are undertaken–interior liberty is increased. This requires the coordination of the spiritual and sensitive faculties in virtues that grant stability and permanence to free choices. The facility and direction granted to acts by virtues develop interior liberty and the quality of personal maturity.[23]

Grace Within the Liberum Arbitrium

The human experience of the weakness of free choice in confrontation with the attractiveness of the objects perceived by the senses, which are capable of obscuring the objective good presented by practical reason, as well as the experience of the escape from liberty because it is demanding in the creativeness of virtue, is a sign of the consequences of original sin. Grace is therefore needed for the development of interior liberty and for the confirmation of choices in good.[24] The mature exercise of the free choice of true good is a sign of the sanctifying divine presence. Man can undertake through free choices that good which is proportionate to his state of fallen nature. But the giving up of all sin and perseverance in that supreme good to which the will is by nature ordained is impossible without grace.[25] The *liberum arbitrium* in the natural state includes the inclination of the will toward the good, but that inclination without grace is insufficiently powerful for a permanent attainment of the good.[26] When, however, free choice is transformed from within by God, it acquires the capacity to choose acts that transcend the power of human nature, like the decision to love one's enemy.[27] Spiritual life consists in the free and creative undertaking of choices that have at their root the support of grace recognized only in faith. Divine grace then elicits in the will virtuous acts that, though made by men, are essentially supernatural.[28]

Because God is the Creator of the human will, he can transform it—and only God can do this—in such a manner that the will itself wills that which is good. Grace ennobles the choice and unites the soul with God.[29] The action of divine love poured out into human hearts by the Holy Spirit who has been given (Romans 5:5) enhances liberty, because the presence of God in the essence of the soul corrects the functioning of reason and will. The supernatural light coming from above to the mind in the gift of wisdom, without depriving reason of its natural capacities and rights, elevates it, bringing out a perspective that is open to the divine mystery. That perspective has an inherent attractiveness about it, even though what is presented cannot be rationally explained and defended because it is based upon the mystery of faith.

Similarly, charity does not inundate the human will with divine love. It draws out of the will its natural inclination for that which the gift of wisdom has presented to reason. This, in turn, elicits joy and peace of heart, which appear whenever the will reposes in its appropriate object. When grace works in the will, it strengthens the attractiveness, the fascination that draws the will. Grace is a liberation of free spontaneity and not the delivery of extra energy for the execution of externally imposed obligations. When the grace of the Holy Spirit is recognized in faith, it restores the original, spontaneous attraction of the will toward that which is good. The disorder of the will to be healed by grace consists of the fact that the will acts against itself, against that which it desires most profoundly, and also in that it acts correctly in accord with its inner need and the enlightening direction of reason, but it interprets this as a burden, because the true, spontaneous attraction of the will is latent. Both of these distortions of the will are corrected from within by the Holy Spirit, who indwells the human soul.[30]

The understanding of the nature of liberty that Aquinas offers shows that, contrary to the common apprehension of the contemporary mind, man is not born with a free will but with an enslaved will. Just as human reason has to be developed with education through which it embraces truth, so the will needs formation in order to adhere to goodness. With the passage of time, the will is exercised, and thanks to the cooperation of grace, it matures, becoming more and more free. The sanctifying presence of God through grace liberates the spiritual faculties, reason, and the will, making them capable of mutual cooperation in the undertaking of truly free acts.

Difficulties Encountered in the Development of the Liberum Arbitrium

The practical functioning of reason and will in acts of free choice, in which the good is chosen with persistence, clarity, and, if needed, with fortitude, requires an appropriate transformation of both reason and will which redirects both these faculties toward what is true and good. Conscience needs to be enlightened and trained, and the will needs to be liberated. Psychology since Sigmund Freud is aware of the sinister consequences of emotional repression that blocks the development of interior liberty and psychological maturity. Much more dangerous, however, in the life of a Christian is the poisoning influence of intellectual and spiritual repression that prevents the flowering of the spiritual faculties in their capacity for the *liberum arbitrium*. Liberation from these forms of repression is necessary for the practical functioning of conscience.

In the repression of emotions, the judgment of conscience is totally, or in part, replaced by an ill-directed feeling. Sensitive cognition and the consequent movement of the feelings may seem to be entitled to be the directing force in action. But these feelings do not belong to the essence of conscience. Emotions are a psychic and carnal reaction to sensitive cognition. At the same time, they have an innate capacity to follow the judgment of reason. The distinction made between the sensitive utility judgment that motivates the emotions and the judgment of reason in conscience that focuses the movement of the emotions toward rationally perceived objectives is necessary for a clear apprehension of the nature of conscience. The repeated direction of the emotions by reason, which presents values, habituates the emotions to virtuous activity. Growth in virtue is a sign of interior liberation, in which the dynamism of emotions is harnessed in the service of the perceived good. The rational judgment that directs the emotions is never experienced by them as being repressive, even though it may often be demanding.

Due to faulty education, however, emotions can neurotically block one another.[31] In a typical case of a person suffering from neurotic repression, an emotion of the concupiscible appetite–the *appetitus concupisibilis*–is blocked by an emotion of the irascible appetite–the *appetitus irascibilis*–that is moved by the sensitive utility judgment in such a manner that the judgment of reason is unable to direct the repressed emotion. In a classical example of sexual repression, whenever the sexual desire is emotionally aroused by some perceived or imagined object, the emotion of fear or the emotion of energy is immediately aroused, which represses the sexual desire. The neurotic person, therefore, cannot control his sexual desire in a rational way because, before any rational direction is given to the desire, it is suppressed by the emotion of fear or by the feeling of obligation. Whenever he feels desire, he immediately feels guilty, and moved by a feeling of obligation or fear, he represses that desire. Such an approach, far from leading to inner liberty and to the virtue of chastity, causes the repressed desire to reappear in an uncontrolled and unfree manner. This, in turn, leads to a further repression, and the vicious circle is continued. The neurotic may be convinced that he is fulfilling his obligation, that the repression is his only defense against sin. He may ascribe the guilty feelings that cause the repression to his conscience, but, in fact, he is in error. It is not his conscience that is guiding him, but his feelings moved by his sensitive utility judgment. There is an essential difference between the guidance of the emotions by conscience, in which the feelings of the emotions are affirmed and rationally directed toward the good that is then chosen by the *liberum arbitrium*, and the repression of the emotions undertaken by other emotions such as fear or the feeling of obligation. It is quite possible to know that a particular emotion or action is morally good or indifferent and, at the same time, feel guilty about it due to an excessive influence of the repressing emotion. Such guilty, though unfounded, feelings, mistaken for the judgment of conscience, cause the repressive process. In fact, they take the place of the judgment of reason, that is, of conscience, and impede the development of interior freedom. Moral teaching, therefore, is to be presented in such a way that it does not elicit unhealthy reactions.

When Freud discovered the repressive process, he ascribed the cause of the emotional disturbance to the superego. He saw, however, the superego as a fusion of conscience, of pressure coming from moral requirements and from the emotions. He was correct in discerning the repressive process, but he was wrong in his interpretation. In neurotic repression it is not conscience or the moral law that is causing the repression. Repression is caused by the blocking of the emotions, in which the emotion of fear or the emotion of energy replaces the rational judgment of conscience. Neither moral law nor reason in its direction of the emotions causes repression. Repression comes from an emotion that is excessively and unnecessarily aroused, which replaces and prevents the rational direction of the emotions.

A sound moral education, therefore, should grant the ability to discern the rational judgment of the conscience and also to differentiate it from feelings of obligation or guilt, which are secondary and justified only if they are in accord with the judgments of reason. To follow one's conscience, one must have confidence in the judgment of conscience, irrespective of the feelings that may accompany it. Since conscience is an act of reason, its judgments can be rationally defended. This confidence in the judgment of conscience is a necessary prerequisite for its functioning, concomitant with the simultaneous need of education of the conscience in truth. A person whose conscience is formed in truth, but who does not have confidence in its judgments, is far from free. Feelings of doubt in the overscrupulous person are caused by an excessive fear that has overtaken the function of reason. This fear has become for him a primary rule of action thereby prohibiting reason from directing activity.

Therefore, it is supremely important to reflect upon the way in which moral law is received. Moral law is fundamentally sapiential. In the vision of Aquinas it is rational, not voluntaristic. Natural law discerns the harmony of things that is intrinsic to creatures, since creation is a gift of the wisdom of God. Revealed moral law, even though it leads us further than the natural mind can envisage, does not appear as contradictory to reason. The receptivity of moral norms is, therefore, to be rational, not emotional. Even though it can lead to obedience to the precepts out of love for the Law-giver, a voluntaristic theory of moral law more often than not leads to an emotional receptivity of moral norms in which either the emotion of fear or the emotion of energy flowing from a resolute feeling of obligation replaces the rational receptivity of moral norms. Such an approach does not lead to inner spiritual liberty. Whenever moral exhortation is violently rejected, the mode of its reception should therefore be checked. If the apprehension of moral law is voluntaristic, causing an emotional reception that requires obedience *ad nutum*, it invariably handicaps the functioning of reason, disabling free choice. This is instinctively recognized and, in a braver personality, causes the rejection of moral exhortation.

Divine guidance, received in faith, is also sapiential and not voluntaristic. The act of faith through which the mystery of God is received in love is humility on the part of reason, but not a denial of reason. The Christian conscience that meets God in faith does not deny the functions or the dignity of reason. The conscience that is open to the divine mystery in faith searches for understanding–*fides quaerens intellectum*–as it issues its practical judgments. Obedience to precepts out of religious motives, therefore, is still to be undertaken by conscience, that is, by reason and not by the emotional feelings of propriety or guilt. Religious obedience, therefore, has to be distinguished carefully from other forms of obedience that can mistakenly deform the Christian. Military obedience consists of a restraint and redirection of the will under the guidance of reason. It is a reasonable thing for a soldier to obey his superiors, particularly in conditions that endanger his life. Communist or totalitarian obedience consists of the repressing of the will and assertive emotions under the dictates of fear. Such obedience deprives the person of his maturity and dignity. Religious obedience consists of the humility of the will directed by faith. It neither deprives the person of his dignity nor does it prevent the acquisition of spiritual maturity. Conscience as the act of reason, when it is enlightened by faith, remains as the interior lord.

The rational functioning of conscience in its reception of truth presented by the norm should also be distinguished from the process of rationalization, that is, the searching for excuses to defend an action that has previously been decided upon. Conscience in its process of discernment functions within the inherent nature of reason, which has a structural inclination for truth. In thereby assessing a situation, it attempts to discern the truth of that situation. A rationalizing mind, however, knows instinctively that the action that has been decided upon is evil, discordant with truth, and that is why, in its perversion, it attempts to invent arguments that would convince itself that the course it has decided upon is acceptable. This procedure of the reflecting reason is knowingly deflecting from the demanding requirements of truth. It is not the true voice of conscience.

The process of emotional repression in its blocking of inner liberty can by analogy be compared to a deformation of the intellect. The espousal of philosophical and ideological positions that incapacitate the mind so that it cannot adhere to truth is a form of intellectual repression. The ideological mind fixes onto a truth or a half-truth and then, blind to wider aspects of reality, attempts to resolve all problems with the one key it possesses. A convinced positivist or Marxist is unable to perceive what for another is plain common sense because the drive of his reason for truth has been repressed. The intellectual ruin caused by ideological domination has justly been termed an enslavement of the mind. An ideological mind, in its pride, attempts to push forward its own understanding of things with the intent of reorganizing the existing reality according to its own vision of the future. The transformation of Christian faith into ideology, whether to the left or the right, is always a proud manipulation of truth that extinguishes the filial relationship with the eternal Father. The fact that in the center of the Christian revelation lies not a message or plan of transformation of this world but the living Person of the Father, with whom a filial relationship can be established, defends the mind of the believer from ceasing to be open to truth. An encounter with a person always leaves room for something new. A mind that is open to a living God is open to the enriching novelty of truth and does not stop short in the net of intellectual repression.

The formation of conscience, therefore, entails the presentation of an intellectual perspective in such a way that is open to the attraction of truth. The all-pervasive intellectual climate with its subjectivity and fright of decided conviction concerning the fundamentals of being and life certainly impedes the capacity of conscience from making lasting decisions. It is not, however, impossible to arrive at such a conviction, because the intellect is endowed with an inclination for truth. The study of elementary philosophy is of great assistance in the development of conscience, on the condition that it leads to truth and not just to an erudite knowledge of conflicting opinions. The attainment of the conviction that the cognition of truth is possible not only in the realm of faith but also rationally is of prime importance. Without such a conviction, the persistent good choice of the *liberum arbitrium* requires a heroic and almost impossible faith.

The third type of repression, that is, the spiritual, is the most nefarious in its consequences. It consists of the blocking of divine charity from within. Charity, habitually present in the person in the state of grace, is unable there to flower in a rich and virtuous personality. To free oneself from this repression, a continual conversion is needed. The soul has to open in faith to the sanctifying presence of the Holy Spirit, which then pours out in practical charity and an apostolic fecundity that build the church from within. Moral theology that focuses on the dynamic presence of God in the sanctified person can open up a perspective that assists in liberation from spiritual repression. The knowledge of theology does not in itself free from repression. The liberation of the soul is a long-term process that requires more than just a rational presentation of the sanctifying divine presence. To reach the summits of spiritual life, in which the divine transforming presence in the soul is operative in all the faculties of the soul, several stages of active and passive purgations are required. But a theology of divinized human action can present a vision of the theandric cooperation that leads to free creativity of charity.

The development of interior liberty that responds to the natural hunger for creativity requires that the three types of repression mentioned (emotional, intellectual, and spiritual) be healed. It is only then that the functioning of the conscience and the will will be appropriate, allowing them to generate truly good acts.

Conclusion

The relationship between conscience and truth, and between freedom and the law, can be studied both from the angle of the acting subject and from the angle of that which is external to the subject. A relationship may be viewed from both its terms. A study of these relationships from the point of view of truth and of moral law may seem to be the only objective approach. What is superior to the acting subject is an objective reality with which he has to measure himself. But a study from the point of view of conscience, the spiritual faculties, and their freedom can also be objective, if the nature of these faculties and the mode of their transformation is taken into account. Does the presentation of moral teaching have to commence with the objective reality that is "out there" and which conditions the acting person from without? Or can it not commence with a study of the acting person, his intrinsic needs, his finality, his search for beatitude, and of the response of God to his hunger?

A theological study of God, who is present through grace in the interior sanctuary of the acting person, grants a line of approach to moral theology that restrains the feeling that human freedom is being limited from without and does not necessarily deny the requirements of the objective reality that is outside the acting person. In this perspective, the presentation of the transforming and liberating presence of God within human acts, as well as the pointing out of sins that destroy the receptiveness to that presence, does not have the tone of imposing moralization. Moral theology is an annunciation, the revelation of the Good News about God, who liberates charity in us and who, through the divine indwelling of the human soul, bestows the liberty in the Holy Spirit that empowers the person to respond in a prudent and creative manner to confronting challenges. Furthermore, the revelation about God, who is attained in the depths of the soul, responds to the innermost desire for happiness that is written into human nature.

The divine influence from within, through grace that is discreet and inviting, and the divine influence from without, through the instruction of the moral law that is sapiential, educate the conscience so that the person is made capable of creative and generous acts of charity. Conscience can be said to have an executive and judiciary power, but not a legislative power. Conscience does not create norms for itself. But like a good administrator who is creative in his ways of serving his country, conscience has to supply the arguments for the free choice of the act. Conscience cannot function like a dull bureaucrat who is afraid to take an initiative not provided for in the rules. Conscience transformed by grace supplies the boost for the *liberum arbitrium*, the free response that, taking into account the demands of objective truth and the guidance of moral norms, retains its initiative and freedom of expression.

Christian teaching of morals is primarily an aid in the supernatural transformation of conscience and free choice that enables the love of God to be made visible in the free and spontaneous acts of human creativity. It is the teaching of the use of freedom that enhances spiritual liberty that ought to be the primary concern of moralists. If moral teaching is interpreted uniquely as a series of precepts and prohibitions, it elicits as a reaction an attempt to defend the sphere of liberty by the total or partial rejection of all norms. In such a reaction, conscience will be set against the moral norms with which it will always be in opposition. If moral teaching presents the ways in which, with divine assistance, personal liberation is developed, the conscience is naturally attracted to it.

I conclude on an optimistic note by stating that the effect of a theology does not depend solely upon the convincing character of the arguments that are proposed. The teaching of the church in the realm of morals can be fruitful only if it is perceived in the light of faith as the secondary element of the law of the Spirit. The new law that primarily consists of the grace of the Holy Spirit also includes the written text of the gospels and the teaching of the church. These written texts are to dispose to faith, and they order the use of grace. A theology that is rooted in the divinely revealed mystery, when it is transmitted in faith, is endowed with a divine fecundity. It generates and nourishes faith and opens the heart to cooperation with grace in the various dimensions of human life and activity. The openness to the present and decisive dynamism of the Holy Spirit is essential for the fruitful transmission of any moral exhortation.

Notes

1. Richard Neuhaus, *Doing Well and Doing Good: The Challenge to the Christian Capitalist,* quotation from the Polish translation: *Biznes i Ewangelia. Wezwanie dla chrzecijanina-kapitalisty* (Pozna: Wdrodze, 1993), p. 174.

2. *VS,* 29.

3. *VS,* 72.

4. *Ia-IIae,* prol.: *Quia, sicut Damascenus dicit, homo factus ad imaginem Dei dicitur, secundum quod per imaginem significatur* intellectuale et arbitrio liberum et per se potestativum; . . . *restat ut consideremus de Eius imagine, idest de homine, secundum quod et ipse est suorum operum principium, quasi liberum arbitrium habens et suorum operum potestatem.*

5. *De Veritate,* q. 24, art. 4: *Et ideo liberum arbitrium habitum non nominat, sed potentiam voluntatis vel rationis, unam siquidem per ordinem ad alteram.*

6. Ibid., art 2: *Cum ad operationem nostram tria concurrunt, scilicet cognitio, appetitus et ipsa operatio, tota ratio libertatis ex modo cognitionis dependet . . . unde totius libertatis radix est in ratione constituta.*

7. Ibid., art. 6, sc. 2: *Electio appetitus est praeconsiliati. . . . Ergo liberum arbitrium est voluntas. c.: Potentia qua libere judicamus, non intelligitur illa qua iudicamus simpliciter, quod est rationis; sed quae facit libertatem in judicando, quod est voluntatis. Unde liberum arbitrium est ipsa voluntas; nominat autem eam non absolute, sed in ordine ad aliquem actum ejus, qui est eligere.*

8. *Ia-IIae,* q. 9, art. 1, ad 3: *Voluntas movet intellectum quantum ad exercitium actus. . . . Sed quantum ad determinationem actus, quae est ex parte obiecti, intellectus movet voluntatem. De Veritate,* q. 24, art. 6, ad 3: *Quamvis judicium sit rationis, tamen libertas judicandi est voluntatis immediate. ad 5: Voluntas quodammodo movet rationem imperando actum ejus, et ratio movet voluntatem proponendo ei objectum suum, quod est finis; et inde est quod utraque potentia potest aliqualiter per aliam informari.*

9. Ibid., art. 1: *Homo vero per virtutem rationis judicans de agendis, potest de suo arbitrio judicare, in quantum cognoscit rationem finis et ejus quod est ad finem, et habitudinem et ordinem unius ad alterum: et ideo non est solum causa sui ipsius in movendo, sed in judicando; et ideo est liberi arbitrii, ac si diceretur liberi judicii de agendo vel de non agendo.*

10. *Ia,* q. 80, art. 2: *Potentia enim appetitiva est potentia passiva, quae nata est moveri ab apprehenso. IIa-IIae,* q. 24, art. 2: . . . *obiectum vero appetitus intellectivi*

vel voluntatis, est bonum sub communi ratione boni, prout est apprehensibile ab intellectu. Ia-IIae, q. 110, art. 1: *Voluntas autem hominis movetur ex bono praeexistente in rebus.*

11. *Ia-IIae,* q. 9, art. 6, ad 3: *Deus movet voluntatem hominis, sicut universalis motor ad universalis obiectum voluntatis, quod est bonum. Et sine hac universali motione homo non potest aliquid velle.*

12. Ibid., q. 10, art. 1: *Hoc autem est bonum in communi, in quod voluntas naturaliter tendit, sicut etiam quaelibet potentia in suum obiectum: et etiam ipse finis ultimus . . . et universaliter omnia illa quae conveniunt volenti secundum suam naturam. Non enim per voluntatem appetimus solum ea quae pertinent ad potentiam voluntatis; sed etiam ea quae pertinent ad singulas potentias, et ad totum hominem. Unde naturaliter homo vult non solum obiectum voluntatis, sed etiam alia quae conveniunt aliis potentiis; ut cognitionem veri, quae convenit intellectui; et esse et vivere et alia huiusmodi, quae respiciunt consistentiam naturalem; quae omnia comprehenduntur sub obiecto voluntatis, sicut quaedam particularia bona.*

13. Ibid., art. 1, ad 3: *Sub bono autem communi multa particularia bona continentur, ad quorum nullum voluntas determinatur. De Veritate,* q. 24, art. 7, ad 6: *Felicitatem indeterminate et in universali omnis rationalis mens naturaliter appetit, et circa hoc deficere non potest; sed in particulari non est determinatus motus voluntatis creaturae ad quaerendam felicitatem in hoc vel illo.*

14. *De Malo,* q. 3, art. 3: *Voluntas ad nihilum ex necessitate movetur quod non appareat habere necessarium connexionem cum beatitudine, quae est naturaliter volita . . . Particularia bona non habent necessarium connexionem cum beatitudine, quia sine quolibet eorum potest homo esse beatus. Unde quantumcumque homini proponatur aliquid eorum ut bonum, voluntas non ex necessitate in illud tendit.*

15. *De Veritate,* q. 24, art. 1, ad 20: I*n appetibilibus, de fine ultimo non judicamus judicio discussionis vel examinationis, sed naturaliter approbamus, propter quod de eo non est electio, sed voluntas. Habemus ergo respectu ejus* liberam voluntatem . . . *non autem liberum judicium, proprie loquendo, cum non cadat sub electione.*

16. *Ia,* q. 62, art. 8, ad 3: . . . *quod liberum arbitrium . . . eligat aliquid divertendo ab ordine finis, quod est peccare, hoc pertinet ad defectum libertatis. Unde maior libertas arbitrii est in angelis, qui peccare non possunt, quam in nobis, qui peccare possumus.*

17. *De Veritate,* q. 24, art. 7: *Nulla creatura nec est, nec esse potest, cujus liberum arbitrium sit naturaliter confirmatum in bono, ut hoc ei ex puris naturalibus conveniat quod peccare non possit.*

18. Ibid., art. 8: *Voluntas enim naturaliter tendit in bonum sicut in suum obiectum; quod autem aliquando in malum tendat, hoc non contingit nisi quia malum sibi sub specie boni proponitur.*

19. Ibid., art 2: *Et quod quandoque appetitus videatur cognitionem non sequi, hoc ideo est, quia non circa idem accipitur appetitus et cognitionis judicium: est enim appetitus de particulari operabili, judicium vero rationis quandoque est de aliquo universali, quod est quandoque contrarium appetitui.*

20. *De Veritate,* q. 17, art. 1, ad 4: . . . *iudicium conscientiae consistit in pura cognitione, iudicium autem liberi arbitrii in applicatione cognitionis ad affectione: quod quidem iudicium est iudicium electionis. Et ideo contingit quandoque quod*

iudicium liberi arbitrii pervertitur, non autem conscientiae; sicut cum aliquis examinat aliquid quod imminet faciendum, et iudicat quasi adhuc speculando per principia, hoc esse malum ... sed quando incipit applicare ad agendum, occurrunt undique multae circumstantiae ad ipsum actum, utpote fornicationis delectatio, ex cuius concupiscentiae ligatur ratio, ne eius dictamen in eius reiectionem prorumpat. Et sic aliquis errat in eligendo, et non in conscientia.

21. *Ia-IIae*, q. 57, art. 5, ad 3: ... *verum intellectus speculativi accipitur per conformitatem intellectus ad rem ... Verum autem intellectus practici accipitur per conformitatem ad appetitum rectum.*

22. *In decem libros ethicorum Aristotelis ad Nicomachum expositio,* l. 6, lect. 2, 1131: ... *appetitum est finis et eorum quae sunt ad finem: finis autem determinatus est homini a natura ... Ea autem quae sunt ad finem, non sunt nobis determinata a natura, sed per rationem investiganda. Sic ergo manifestum est quod rectitudo appetitus per respectu ad finem est mensura veritatis in ratione practica. Et secundum hoc determinatur veritas rationis practicae secundum concordiam ad appetitum rectum. Ipsa autem veritas rationis practicae est regula rectitudinis appetitus circa ea quae sunt ad finem.*

23. *De Veritate,* q. 24, art. 1, ad 19: ... *in potestate animae rationalis sit accipere, vel etiam refutare passiones subortas. Postmodum vero homo efficitur aliqualis per aliquem habitum acquisitum, cujus nos causa sumus, vel infusum, qui sine nostro consensu non datur, quamvis ejus causa non simus. Et ex hoc habitu efficitur quod homo efficaciter appetat finem consonum illi habitui; at tamen ille habitus necessitatem non inducit, nec libertatem electionis non tollit.*

24. *De Veritate,* q. 24, art. 8: ... *liberum arbitrium per gratiam potest confirmari in bono.*

25. *De Veritate,* q. 24, art. 14: *Ad hoc ergo bonum quod est supra naturam humanam, constat liberum arbitrium non posse sine gratia. ... Illud autem bonum quod est naturae humanae proportionatum, potest homo per liberum arbitrium explere.* Art. 12, ad 1: ... *non potest homo peccator facere sine gratia ut vitet omnia peccata mortalia, quamvis possit vitare singula; et sic non potest sine gratia voluntatem naturalem implere; et similiter est de justo, respectu peccatorum venialium.*

26. Ibid., art. 10, ad 1: ... *quia habet naturalem inclinationem in illud, quamvis in se non habeat sufficiens illius principium ex quo necessario consequatur.*

27. Ibid., art. 12, ad sc. 6: *Liberum arbitrium potest habere electionem et consilium non solum de illis ad quae sufficit propria potestas, sed de illis ad quae indiget divino auxilio.*

28. *Ia-IIae*, q. 109, art. 5, ad 1: ... *homo sua voluntate facit opera meritoria vitae aeternae: sed ... ad hoc exigitur quod voluntas homini praeparetur a Deo per gratiam.* *IIa-IIae*, q. 23, art. 2: *Non enim motus caritatis ita procedit a Spiritu Sancto movente humanam mentem quod humana mens sit mota tantum et nullo modo sit principium huius motus, sicut cum aliquid corpus movetur ab aliquo exteriori movente. Hoc enim est contra rationem voluntarii, cuius oportet principium in ipso esse. ... Sed oportet quod sic voluntas moveatur a Spiritu Sancto ad diligendum quod etiam ipsa sit efficiens hunc actum.*

29. Ibid., art. 8, ad 6: *Gratia secundum esse suum est in libero arbitrio per modum ejus sicut accidens in subjecto; sed tamen ad rationem suae immutabilitatis liberum arbitrium pertrahit, ipsum Deo conjungens.*

30. *Summa contra Gentiles,* l. 4, c. 22, (3589): *Cum Spiritus Sanctus per amorem voluntatem inclinet in verum bonum, in quo naturaliter ordinatur, tollit et servitutem qua, servus passionis et peccati effectus, contra ordinem voluntatis agit, et servitutem qua, contra motum suae voluntatis, secundum legem agit, quasi legis servus, non amicus.*

31. For a Thomistic interpretation of neurosis cf. Anna A. Terruwe and Conrad W. Baars, *Psychic Wholeness and Healing* (New York: Alba House, 1981).

4

Conscience, Truth, and Prudence

SERVAIS PINCKAERS, O.P.

As stated in Cardinal Ratzinger's article, "Conscience and Truth," the central problem encountered in moral theology at the present time is the relation between conscience and truth. Is our personal conscience the ultimate judge of the truth of our acts? Is it their very source? Or, is our conscience the witness within us of a superior truth perceived as a voice, a lawgiving light? In a word, is it a consciousness of truth? This question coincides with the pivotal point of the encyclical *Veritatis Splendor*. Our freedom is not an absolute; it is a freedom for truth; it grows and fulfills itself while serving the truth of which moral law is the expression. The love of truth, at the core of freedom and conscience, is certainly the most profound, the most decisive point of the present moral debate.

Our Heritage: Moral Doctrine on the Commandments and on Virtue

To present clearly the problem of the relation among freedom, conscience, and truth and see its implications, it is useful to study the moral heritage we have received. Catholic teaching on morals comprises two traditions, which have produced two systems of thought. Modern tradition, of which the manuals are the classic expression, introduced the treatise on conscience in place of the treatise on virtue in fundamental moral theology. Special moral theology was divided following questions based on the Ten Commandments, considered as the expression of natural law for which conscience is the witness and the interpreter.

One tradition covers the study of acts, of cases of conscience, and the obligations determined by law or norms, as we say today. It is likened to the moral imperatives in the tradition of Kant. The theological virtues are doubtlessly mentioned in the manuals but serve in fact only as categories under which obligations and sins are listed. The study of virtue was left to ascetical theology in keeping with the search for perfection, which goes beyond the limit of right and wrong proper to morality.

The other tradition, a much older one, which claims its beginnings with the church Fathers and found in St. Thomas its finest systematic expression, builds Christian morality on the theological and moral virtues, perfected by the gifts of the Holy Spirit. The practical virtue par excellence, which leads the moral judgment to its conclusion, is prudence rather than conscience, as in the other tradition.

We find in St. Thomas, however, a conjunction between, on the one hand, the virtue of prudence, analyzed through the resources of the Aristotelian tradition, with the contribution of the monastic tradition of discernment, and on the other, the doctrine of conscience from St. Paul and the Church Fathers, especially St. Jerome. Two levels can be distinguished: *synderesis*, defined as the *habitus* of the first principles of practical reason, and conscience itself, understood by the Angelic Doctor as the act of applying these principles in concrete actions. Having said that, prudence plays incontestably the main role here on the practical level; conscience works for prudence.

It is important to consider the placing of conscience in the organization of moral doctrine in the one view or the other, because its role and even its conception depend on its relation to the other elements of the system.

The Freedom of Indifference and Conscience

But let us return to our problem: the relation among freedom, conscience, and truth. The manual tradition was explicitly linked to the freedom of indifference, as the choice between opposites, for or against. This resulted in a certain opposition, an exteriority between freedom and law. Freedom and law can be compared to two landlords who are contesting the field of human behavior. The moralists say, "Possidet lex, possidet libertas," conscience is seen as the intermediary between law and freedom like a judge in court. It applies law to human acts. Conscience speaks in the name of the law, but it resides in the subject to whom it dictates the law. And so, that is why it can easily fluctuate between a zeal for the law, capable of turning into rigorism, and excessive concern for the subject, which can lead to laxity. The whole argument on probabilism lies in this fluctuation. We see today the pendulum of conscience, which once held firmly to the side of the moral law, forcefully swinging to the side of freedom as the criterion of moral values, so much so that some moralists are beginning to consider that which favors freedom as itself the criterion of moral law.

In this tradition freedom of indifference has given rise to a moral voluntarism that, beginning with freedom as the source of choice, communicates to the law itself understood as the pure will of the divine legislator. It does not allow for complete awareness of the role of truth in moral actions. On one side we have a will that dictates and makes the law, and on the other, a will that obeys. Between the two, it is the function of conscience to make known the commands and imperatives but not to explain them or to give any reasons, because the sole reason is the will of the legislator. Therefore, obedience to the law imposed by conscience through the force of obligation becomes the main virtue in this conception of morality because it exercises a general role. It gives moral form to all acts, even to all virtues. Current claims in favor of freedom and personal conscience are the exact opposite of this conception. They indicate the passage of the will of the legislator to the will of the subject as the principal dynamic within the individual conscience.

The Freedom for Excellence

The encyclical *Veritatis Splendor* wished to reestablish firmly the bonds among freedom, conscience, and truth and to show that truth frees us and favors the growth of true freedom and that consequently the law, with conscience as a manifestation of moral truth, helps form freedom and exercises over it a pedagogical role.

Using these terms, the encyclical follows the tradition of a conception of freedom analyzed by St. Thomas. He received it from the Greek philosophers and the Church Fathers. It can be called a freedom of quality or excellence. It can be defined as a power to carry out acts of quality that are perfect in their order. This freedom is rooted in the natural inclinations proper to our spiritual nature created in the image of God. These are the inclinations to truth, goodness, happiness, and life in society, associated with the inclinations toward the preservation of human beings and to the gift of life.[1] We are dealing with a freedom of attraction and not one of indifference. It proceeds from the aspiration to truth and goodness; it is fundamentally a freedom for what is true and good. As such, it is a participation in Divine freedom.

These inclinations are the basis for the natural law, which presides over the development of human freedom, one could say the development of personality. They provide the first principles for moral judgment in the application of positive acts that are the work of reason. These are also the principles that *synderesis* makes known to us and which direct the judgment of conscience.

Let us note that in this conception of freedom, intellect and will stand together at the source of what we call free will, and that reason and affectivity go to form the choosing that is its proper activity. There is no longer any question of voluntarism. Reason, which grasps truth precisely as the real good, plays an essential part in choice. Practical judgment is inseparable from choice. Intelligence has, equally, a part in the elaboration of the law, which is the work of wisdom, as well as in obedience, which requires the discernment of prudence.

Freedom for Charity

Freedom, as a power to accomplish acts of quality that are true and good, is given to us as a seed. Under the impulsion of natural inclinations it tends to develop progressively, as a spiritual growth.

At the origin of this growth is a spontaneous attraction for truth, goodness, happiness, an inclination toward life in human community. It also comes from a sense of the well-being of others, which in real terms signifies a certain natural love of God and neighbor prior to all instruction. St. Basil could say at the outset of his Rule (Qu.2) that the love of God, like our affection for our parents, is unteachable, *adidaktos.* It is so spontaneous that no schooling is necessary to learn it; it precedes all teaching. Love of God cannot be taught. No one taught us to enjoy the light of day, or to cling to life above all, or to love those who brought us into the world. In the same manner, or even in a stronger way, exterior instruction does not teach us to love God. The very nature of the human being contains a seed that possesses the principle of this ability to love. It is at the school of the commandments of God that this seed should be gathered, cultivated diligently, nourished with care, and brought to fulfillment through Divine grace.

We have a natural basis for receiving charity. It precedes any exterior intervention in the form of an obligation or a prohibition. On this basis we can build a morality of charity in which it is both the principle and the form: as principle, it inspires free acts; as form, it is the force that guides the other virtues toward their ultimate end.

The encyclical introduces an important change in the interpretation of the Decalogue. The Ten Commandments are not reduced to a code of obligations imposed by God. Rather, they are presented as a gift of his wisdom and mercy, demanding a response of love.[2] Since charity is grafted on the natural love of which we have just spoken, it remains the principle of the moral life, even before that of moral obligation. In other terms, the encyclical changes the cornerstone of moral life. Morality must be built on the greatness of love rather than on a legal-type obedience, as was the case in the manuals of moral theology. It was left to spiritual theology to talk about the virtue's growth and perfection.

Freedom, as a capacity to act on our own according to truth and goodness, is given as a seed. It is ourself, our being, our spiritual nature. How can we develop it?

Law, Necessary for the Growth of Freedom

First of all, we need law to guide us in our consideration, especially in the first phase of our moral growth. Law has a unique place for us. It is both exterior and interior, superior and immanent. Moral law comes to us from above and may even be surrounded by thunder and lightning, as on Mount Sinai. However, it corresponds precisely to the dictates of our natural inclinations to truth, goodness, and our intimate sense of God and others. It is exactly what we perceive in our conscience when the voice of God resounds, when divine light shines in the depth of our soul. We can say that this law, even though it is proclaimed exteriorly, even though it is chiseled on stone tablets, is nonetheless inscribed in the heart of man. As written in *Gaudium et Spes*: "Deep within his conscience man discovers a law which he himself has not laid upon himself but which he must obey. Its voice, ever calling him to long to do what is good and to avoid evil, tells him inwardly at the right moment: do this, shun that. For man has in his heart a law inscribed by God."[3]

The Religious Dimension of Law and Conscience

Let us remark also with the encyclical, concerning the moral question asked by the rich young man, that law, like conscience which bears it witness, has a spiritual and ecclesial dimension. Whether it be from the top of Mount Sinai or from the depths of the heart of man, moral law comes from God, from his wisdom and his holiness. It is addressed to those whom it touches in its sense of what is true and good in order to make them part of the People of God. Conscience, therefore, is part of the movement of man's aspiration toward God in company with "those who seek justice." They receive the cultural and religious legacy contained in scripture and stored in human wisdom.

A passage from Newman can be cited here on the Christian conception of conscience. A part of it is given in *The Catechism of the Catholic Church*:

> This at least, is how I read the doctrine of Protestants as well as Catholics. The rule and measure of duty is not utility, not the happiness of the greatest number, nor State convenience, nor fitness, order and the *pulchrum*. Conscience is not a long-sighted selfishness, nor a desire to be consistent with oneself; but it is a messenger from Him, who both in nature and in grace, speaks to us behind a veil and teaches and rules by his representatives.

Conscience is the aboriginal Vicar of Christ, a prophet in its information, a monarch in its peremptoriness, a priest in its bless-
ings and anathemas, and, even though the eternal priesthood
throughout the Church could cease to be, in it the sacerdotal principle would remain and would have a sway.[4]

The Necessity of Virtue

However, law and conscience are not sufficient in order to develop
fully in us the power to act according to the truth and the good that
for us is the freedom of quality. It is the particular work of the virtues
to direct the natural inclinations.

We must give to the word *virtue* its original meaning. It has been
impoverished and deformed through a particular usage by the school
of obligation-based morality. Virtue became the habit of submitting
to the law and, from that point, it turned into boring conformism. But
there is nothing more surprising and fresh than real virtue. It is comparable to the talent of the artist or the excellence of the craftsman. It
possesses a lucidity and an energy that contribute to the perfection of
our most personal ability to act. Proceeding from within us, it makes
us independent with respect to the outside world. Virtue develops our
natural inclinations toward truth and goodness. It gives us the power
to accomplish excellent works for ourselves and for many others and
thereby participate in the creative and providential power of God
according to our capacity and with his help.

Thus, a virtue-based morality covering all the active qualities that
man acquires through intellectual, moral, and spiritual faculties comes
from his natural inclination to goodness and truth, the source of his
freedom.

Morality of Virtues

For a long time, virtue-based morality was predominant in the
church. It was developed gradually from Holy Scripture in conjunction with human and Christian experience. In Greek and Latin philosophy, starting from the question of happiness, which covers all the
natural inclinations, morality was ordered around the four cardinal

virtues: prudence, justice, fortitude, and temperance, already present in the Book of Wisdom. Taken up by the Church Fathers, the doctrine of the virtues became part of a new system governed by the theological virtues of faith, hope, and charity as taught by St. Paul. Accordingly, the significance and reality of virtue was profoundly transformed by this Christian integration. It was no longer formed by human effort but accepted as a gift from God; it is both infused and acquired, passive and active.

It was St. Thomas who would give the morality of the virtues their most authoritative systematizaton, which became the classic one. To give a complete account of the teachings of revelation and Christian experience, and inspired by the writings of St. Augustine, he combined the virtues with the gifts of the Holy Spirit as well as the Beatitudes and the fruits of the Holy Spirit, which St. Paul enumerated in Galatians 5:22. *The Catechism of the Catholic Church* restated this doctrine in the section on virtue, which follows the teaching on conscience and precedes the treatment of sin.[5] St. Thomas divided the study of morality into the theological and cardinal virtues, adding for each one the study of the corresponding gift of the Holy Spirit and relevant Beatitude. After that, sins against the virtues are examined as well as the commandment pertaining to each case.

Prudence as the Link Between the Virtues

When expounded and studied in all its detail, the morality of virtues appears rich and complex. It must be noted, however, that all the virtues, regardless of their number and diversity, form a whole, which is similar to our body with its members and organs. They all act together when we carry out a concrete act. It is here that we meet prudence, and it is here that we can perceive its role and its relation to conscience.

In his analytical expose on the virtues, St. Thomas made clear that they were connected and thus worked together. He showed how this connection was guaranteed by charity and prudence.[6] Charity unites the virtues by ordering them to God, our ultimate end and our complete happiness. Charity enables us to love him with all our heart, all our strength, all our virtues. Prudence, on the other hand, the virtue of practical reason, takes up the other end of the chain. It governs each concrete action and fulfills its function of judgment for all the other virtues, including the theological ones. Prudence discerns *hic et nunc*, according to the circumstances, what is best in order to practice each virtue in its particular place. St. Anthony taught this to his followers when he asked them which virtue could save the monk from the devil's snares and help him rise to the summits of perfection. St. Anthony said that without discernment all the other virtues go astray, to the left or to the right by excessive fervor or by laxity.[7]

Here again, we must give back its original and powerful significance to an old word that has been worn out and distorted. *Prudence* is not a safe or tutiorist ("protectionist") virtue stemming from fear of breaking the law. It is the virtue of discernment, of decision, of action. Prudence does not consist only in careful deliberation or wise advice. Its proper action is what St. Thomas calls the precept that follows choice, that is, the decision which produces the action.[8] It is by this positive and active choice that prudence directs the acts of the other virtues to their end. This, then, is the concept of prudence that we can compare with conscience.

Synderesis, *Conscience, and Prudence*

Before comparing conscience and prudence, let us look upstream at their source. It is all the more useful since St. Thomas's analytical study can tend to hide their natural union due to differences he distinguished in his definitions.

Let us begin with conscience. It originates in the natural and primitive light of *synderesis*, which St. Thomas defines as the *habitus* of the first principles of practical reason. There is a sense of good and evil bound to the very nature of the human spirit. Conscience is found at the conjunction of these two spiritual faculties according to the measure of their inclination to truth and goodness.

Since it belongs "to the very nature of the soul," this light is permanent and unchanging. Its function is to condemn evil and tend toward the good. It provides the primary basis for our moral judgments and cannot err. It enlightens all mankind and is indestructible, regardless of the sins and errors that veil and darken it in our heart.[9] *Synderesis* is therefore the original source of all judgments of conscience. They are the reflection of this original light in the distinctiveness of our actions and all they involve.

Let us stop and make two brief remarks. First, note the importance of the doctrine of *synderesis* in the recent debate. It offers a solid base for the recognition of the universal and permanent character of moral laws coming from within us in the form of a light that illuminates our intellect. The strength of moral law derived from this light does not come to man from a merely exterior will; it has its roots in man's intellect and is at the origin of his freedom.

Second, it is regrettable that the word *synderesis* is so foreign to our modern languages. This is due in part to the weakness of our vocabulary, bound as it is to the experience of the senses and lacking words to designate the deeper and higher realities; it is too often reduced to using abstract and technical terms. Cardinal Ratzinger has suggested the substitution of the word *synderesis* with the word *anamnesis* and has given good reasons to support his suggestion. It can be debated. It is very difficult, however, to replace such a classical term.

To better understand the meaning of *synderesis*, an image given by St. Thomas can be helpful. St. Jerome, in his commentary on Ezekiel's vision of the four animals, spoke of *synderesis* as the "spark of conscience" that was not quelled even in the heart of Cain after his crime. He compared it to the eagle who corrects from above when reason and sensitivity err. They are symbolized in his vision by man, the lion, and the bull. St. Thomas went to the trouble of explaining St. Jerome's comparison and made the distinction between the spark, the purest part of fire, which shoots out above the flame, and the fire itself, which is mixed with alien matter that alters its purity. The spark is *synderesis*, the pure light of truth; the fire is conscience, which can err accidentally by attaching itself to a particular object that is inferior to reason.[10] *Synderesis* is, strictly speaking, the spark of conscience, the origin of the light that illuminates it.

Let us look at prudence. The Thomistic doctrine of prudence directly follows the Aristotelian tradition in its analysis of the faculties and the virtues. Prudence is the specific moral virtue particular to practical reason, but it is not so in an isolated manner. Prudence uses all the data provided by moral science. It is worth clarifying that this science, insofar as it is a virtue, is anterior to prudence and that it directs prudence just as acquired knowledge guides the judgment. Moreover, like knowledge, prudence draws its wisdom from the *habitus* of the first principles of practical reason, which it applies in concrete behavior, that is to say, *synderesis.* Conscience and prudence, therefore, share the same source of light and join in the same work, the elaboration of moral judgment. What is it, then, from that moment which distinguishes them, particularly in an author like St. Thomas, who associates both of them even though he studies them separately?

Comparison Between Conscience and Prudence: How They Differ and How They Converge

St. Thomas, to our knowledge, did not explicitly compare prudence and conscience, but he did analyze them so specifically that it is easy to establish their differences.

First, the passage pertinent to our question is the answer given to an objection in *De Veritate* (q.17, a.1, ad 4), where Thomas compares the judgment of conscience and the choice of the free will. The latter contains practical judgment, which is part of reason and therefore part of prudence, in the choice. There is, however, the following difference: the judgment of conscience remains at the level of knowledge, whereas the judgment of the choosing as well as the judgment of prudence includes the involvement of the "appetite," of affective will. Prudence, in fact, as we have seen, is not content to deliberate, to counsel, to judge in the abstract. Its distinctive action is the command, that is, the decision to act, which necessarily includes the participation of the will. Such is the practical judgment where prudence finds its fulfillment. And that is why it is not only an intellectual virtue but a moral one; prudence can ensure the connection between the other moral virtues. Conscience, on the other hand, although it judges the moral quality of our behavior, is not a virtue; it is the application of *synderesis* in the appraisal of acts we have carried out or will carry out.

This difference should not prevent us from seeing the close collaboration of prudence and conscience. They are two beacons that join and penetrate one another to produce good actions.

Another difference: St. Thomas was the heir to a tradition whereby conscience was bound to the idea of obligation with regard to the law.

A demonstration of this is the way the Angelic Doctor asks the question about erroneous conscience in the *Summa*. He makes an equivalence, asking whether erroneous conscience creates an obligation and if the will that disagrees with mistaken reason is evil, with the aim of bringing the problem of conscience back to that of reason, which he had very carefully studied, following Aristotle. In spite of the similarity, the perspective is rather different. Legal obligations bear directly on exterior acts and determine "that without which no virtue is possible" or the minimum required of everyone. Virtue is a principle interior to our actions and tends spontaneously toward the quality and perfection of action. Conscience sees action within the limits of what is obligatory, but prudence sees action in view of its perfection.

The difference between the two is reduced to a nuance in St. Thomas, who places law at the service of virtue, but it became decisive when nominalism concentrated moral theology strictly on what was legally compulsory. Soon after that, the moralists introduced into fundamental moral theology a treatise on conscience that replaced the treatise on virtues by the treatise on prudence. Conscience became the authority of moral judgment in the subject faced with freedom. Moralists had at this point great difficulty in defining the role of prudence.

A third difference: The judgment of conscience is concerned with past actions. It carries with it either an accusation and so causes remorse, or an approval and thus excuses. On future actions it either incites or forbids on the strength of obligation.[11] But prudence, after having deliberated on the action to be carried out and perhaps calling to mind past experience, is directly concerned with the present moment of the action, because it is through the decision that it brings the action into being in a particular way. It is perhaps why St. Thomas directly associates solicitude or vigilance with prudence, similar to the active attention to the present.[12]

Whatever may be said of these differences, it is clear that the Angelic Doctor saw conscience and prudence as two converging lights coming from the same source. Both are prompted by our aspiration to the truth and both share the object of the discernment between good and evil. They are located on two different levels. Prudence goes beyond mere knowledge in order to enter into our actions and direct them toward truth. Both will come up against the problem of error, which can always affect human judgment in contingent realities like the circumstances of an action.

Prudence and the Formation of Conscience

By associating prudence and conscience in the establishment of moral truth, consideration of the former sheds important light on what we call the formation of conscience. The doctrine on virtue provides us with a classification that is not included by the moralists of conscience. We can show this in two ways.

First, the doctrine on virtue implies the idea of growth, distinguishable in different stages of education, based on the model of the growth of charity described by St. Thomas. He distinguishes among beginners, the proficient, and the perfect.[13] Two main elements contribute to this growth; the help of teachers and the acquiring of personal experience.

Prudence, like all virtue, needs outside assistance in the form of teachers, authorities, or other intermediaries, especially in the first phase of its growth. These people inculcate by word and example, the rudiments of prudence, the principles of good behavior that transmit the heritage of wisdom and culture of a religious or secular kind. Prudence develops thanks to the assimilation of what we acquire from our cultural milieu or from revelation, as in the case of the Ten Commandments. The progressive formation of the virtue of prudence benefits conscience and gives it a solid base and greater clarity as to the difference between good and evil or what is compulsory or forbidden.

The second element that contributes to growth is especially obvious in the second phase (proficient), when personal experience is acquired which calls for our own initiative and a prolonged commitment in keeping with the virtues. It is here that knowledge develops connaturally through repeated contact with the very substance of the action, whether perceptible or spiritual, whether concerning things or persons. It is the fruit of the just and lawful experience of the work of human hands and of the Spirit. This type of knowledge is different from that acquired by reason or observation. It would be preferable to call it wisdom. Connatural knowledge is particularly important in moral theology because it is synthetic and intuitive, and because of that, it is suitable in the forming of judgments of action that require the facts to be grasped in their entirety and discernment as to the order to be given to them. It is, at the same time, a picture of the whole and a view that unites and finalizes.

Connatural knowledge aims directly at progress by the quality and excellence of our action. Nonetheless, it enlightens conscience in the discernment of what is or is not in conformity with the moral law and its obligations: it helps in guaranteeing a fruitful application of *synderesis*, a real participation in its light, a true echo of the voice of God. Furthermore, conscience can be attributed with a directional role that goes beyond legal obligations and can help in the choice of a career, in a conversion, or in a vocation, as seems to be the case with Cardinal Newman. Conscience is then an inner light guiding along the way of truth. The ordinary sense, however, in moral theology links conscience with the obligations set by law.

The conjunction between prudence and conscience appears to be the best way to explain the formation of conscience, which is required in order that it be faithful to the truth; this is because of the development of prudence, which is the specific virtue of the truth in action. We can see, therefore, that conscience and prudence are the organs of truth within us. They become deficient, distorted, or corrupt as soon as their connection with the truth is weakened or broken.

Notes

1. Cf. VS, no. 51, and reference to *Summa Theologiae*, Ia IIae, q.94, a.2.
2. VS, no. 11.
3. *Gaudium et Spes*, no. 16.
4. John H. Newman, *Letter to the Duke of Norfolk*, ch. 5.
5. *The Catechism of the Catholic Church*, part 3, ch. 1, art. 7, nos. 1803-45.
6. *Summa Theologiae*, Ia IIae, q.65.
7. Cassien, 2d conference *Discernment*, ch. 2.
8. *IIa IIae*, q.47, a.8.
9. *Quaestio Disputata de Veritate*, q. 16, a.3.
10. *Q.D. de Veritate*, q.17, a.2, ad 3.
11. *Q.D. de Veritate*, q.17, a.1.
12. *Ia IIae*, q.47, a.9.
13. *Ia IIae*, q.24, a.9.

5

Conscience and the Object of the Moral Act

RALPH MCINERNY

In one of the more moving passages of Mark Twain's *Huckleberry Finn*, Huck decides that, though it is wrong to help a slave escape, he will do so even if he burns in hell for it. I suspect that most readers regard this as an instance of the common moral sense overcoming an evil convention. Surely God won't punish Huck for going against received opinion and helping Jim flee his owner?

And I suppose the novel is open to a number of interpretations at this point. Maybe the episode should be interpreted as Huck's rejection of the notion that one human person can be the property of another, a rejection that would then free him from any obligation flowing from the institution of slavery. The scene would then depict Huck altering his conscience from an erroneous to a true one. Well, maybe. But let's imagine that we have a pure case. And he means what he says. Huck accepts slavery and thereby his obligation not to aid an owner's property from getting away from him. Nonetheless, overwhelmed by his affection for Jim, he decides to act contrary to his conviction, even if it means eternal damnation.

We may be reminded here of Aristotle's mention of the sophistic attempt to show that folly combined with moral weakness is virtue.

Aristotle writes–in English, as he sometimes does–"This is the way it runs: if a man is both foolish and morally weak, he acts contrary to his conviction because of his moral weakness; but because of his folly, his conviction is that good things are bad and he ought not to do them. Therefore, acting contrary to his conviction, he will do what is good and not what is bad."[1]

The human act embodies a singular judgment that to do this particular thing here and now is good because it is an instance of an act of a certain kind. That is, practical discourse can be seen as the appraisal of the circumstances in which the agent finds himself in the light of a general opinion or principle as to how one ought to act.[2] On the level of generality, there are principles and precepts expressing ways of acting that are always or usually *ut in pluribus* good. But, as Aristotle remarks, no one becomes good *philosophando,* by thinking correctly at a level of generality.[3] Rather, the singular circumstances have to be thought of along with *con-scientia,* in the light of, the general knowledge.

A judgment of conscience dictates that to do such and such here and now is the right thing to do, or that not to do such and such here and now would be wrong. To act contrary to this judgment is, by definition, to do what one thinks is wrong. Conscience then binds, because it does not permit us to act well if we act contrary to its judgment.

That conscience binds even when it is erroneous, however, appears to relativize the proximate rule of conduct, freeing it of objective truth or falsity. For does it not seem that what I think to be the right thing to do *is* the right thing to do, and that this is why to act contrary to the judgment vitiates my act even though, objectively, I do no evil? The objection may indeed be pressed to the point of calling into question any objective standard by reference to which the individual conscience could be called erroneous. It is only by being subjectively adopted that the "objectively correct judgment" can measure my act, the objector might insist. This voids of sense, he holds, the very notion of an erroneous conscience, with the result that every judgment of conscience is correct. To invoke what I might think, if I thought otherwise than I do, does not affect the fact that then as now I am bound to act in accordance with what I think. Morality, it thus appears, is radically subjective, and there is no need, indeed no possibility, of invoking objective norms.

In order to counter this kind of radical relativizing, we must be able to say that, while I am always bound to act in accord with my conscience, on penalty of acting wrongly, nonetheless, to act in accord with my conscience is not always to act rightly. If, on the one hand, the radical relativizing of conscience, with the consequent rejection of the notion of an erroneous conscience, entails that to act in accord with one's conscience is always to act rightly, on the other hand, to retain the notion of an erroneous conscience entails that the agent cannot then avoid acting wrongly. If he fails to act in accord with his erroneous conscience, he acts wrongly, but if he acts in accord with an erroneous conscience he also acts wrongly. Such a one would seem to be, in Thomas's term, *perplexus*, in a moral dilemma, damned if he does and damned if he doesn't.

In what follows, I shall discuss (1) the link between conscience and general principles; (2) how conscience binds; (3) deliberation and conscience, *consilium* and conscience, and (4) St. Thomas's version of Newman's toast to conscience.

Conscience and First Principles

It is a small but important logical point that those who disagree must be in agreement. Of course they agree on some things and disagree on others, but without a backdrop of agreement the disagreement would be impossible. (This is a particular instance of the truth that in order to differ things must in some way be the same.) You and I may disagree as to which of Henry James's novels is the best, agreeing as we do that James was indeed the master of the novel in English, but there are benighted souls who disagree, who find James prolix, oblique, and dull, and who recommend Erle Stanley Gardner. And, of course, Gardner fans may disagree about which of the Perry Mason cases is best.

The logical point that disagreement presupposes agreement gets quickly swallowed up in diversity: diversity of taste, topics, and terrain. If we had hoped it meant that there are certain things on which all humans agree, we may feel the twinge of disappointment. But that larger claim *can* be made. There are certain truths that cannot be gainsaid, truths on which all perforce agree, and agreement we might say is the very condition of disagreement.

When he took up this matter, Aristotle fittingly drew attention to the shared language in which we express our disagreements. He imagined someone persisting in the claim that something can be true and false at the same time and deftly applied this to the claim itself, thereby causing it to effervesce. His point was that in order to *say* the opposite of the very first principle, I must invoke that principle, so either I am stupid or willful in denying it. In either case, I lose the right to be heeded.

That there are things that anyone and everyone in principle knows is not confined to descriptive or theoretical claims; the same can be said of the moral order. There are starting points to moral discourse that everyone in principle already knows. Thomas calls the having of this unlearned moral knowledge *synderesis* and its content natural law.[4]

This is an amazing claim. Is it plausible? On the face of it, given the widespread and deep-seated disagreements among persons of the same culture, to say nothing of the diversity obtaining between cultures, and given additionally a diachronic factor, it must seem Pickwickian to claim that there are certain moral principles on which all agree. But this is precisely what appeal to a natural moral law entails.

Sometimes, the task for the proponent of natural law is seen to be one of seeking and finding ways of persuading others to adopt natural law principles. But if there is a natural law, the interlocutor already holds it, and the task is to elicit from him the recognition that he already does, that there are principles common to him and to everyone else.[5] To discuss natural law on any other basis, I believe, would be to deny it; there are no prior, more common principles to which appeal could be made in an effort to persuade another to adopt natural law principles.[6]

It is nonetheless well to introduce talk of these principles in terms of disagreement, since nothing seems to characterize human society more than disagreement about what is or is not to be done. The reminder that agreements lurk behind such disagreements should not be taken to mean that it is the work of a summer's day to draw them out. Moral relativists and nihilists will very likely regard efforts to elicit the moral absolutes to which they covertly and subconsciously subscribe as some kind of linguistic legerdemain. It is one thing to argue that disagreement about the death penalty is profitably discussed by making explicit the principles of justice on which the disputants are in agreement. It is quite another thing to show that the libertine and the chaste man, whatever their disagreements about womanizing, are in agreement about the need to moderate the pursuit of pleasure. The case for natural law, understood as principles every human agent already in principle accepts, often requires a painstaking dialectical process that is forever in danger of being aborted.[7]

Synderesis is said to urge us to the good and to warn us against evil (*remurmurare malo et inclinare ad bonum*). It does this by making judgments as to what is good and what is bad. Its judgments, those of *synderesis*, natural law, are universal, general, and are contrasted with the judgment of choice, which is particular.[8] This is how conscience is distinguished from *synderesis*: it applies the common principles to particular deeds.[9]

Conscience, then, is a particular judgment as to what is to be done in the light of a common principle. The term means the *act* of application, but *conscience* can also mean the judgment made, as when someone tells us *what* his conscience tells him.

Cardinal Ratzinger, in a paper that was addressed to the American bishops a few years ago, observes that, despite this traditional distinction between *synderesis* (he suggests calling it *anamnesis*) and conscience, usage has changed; now *conscience* has come to mean both the general principles and the particular application of them. I think, actually, both uses are found in St. Thomas, so it's not all that recent, but it's certainly common now. This is an important point that Cardinal Ratzinger makes. While an appeal to one's conscience might be a stopper if by this is meant the particular judgment, such an appeal cannot close off discussion if by conscience is meant general principles, a judgment as to what one *ought* to do. For example, someone who says that his conscience tells him it is all right to practice contraception may indeed be truly reporting that he thinks this, but it would be odd to assume that this makes *what* he thinks immune to discussion. Presumably, he means the practice is all right for others as well as for himself, and this general claim can and ought to be discussed. So conscience in one of the senses, the traditional sense of an application to the here and now, is a stopper. I mean, if somebody says, "That's the way I see it," it's pretty hard to know on what basis we may disagree with him. Whereas if someone says, "My conscience tells me . . ." and fills in the blank with a general statement about how human beings may act, then that's open to discussion and is not a stopper.

That Conscience Always Binds

Our opening discussion invoked as a given that the judgment of conscience always binds. This metaphor suggests, as Thomas notes, necessity. We must obey our conscience. Whence comes this necessity? Earlier, I made this a kind of analytic point. If my judgment of conscience dictates that such and such an act is what I must now do on penalty of acting wrongly, then, definitionally as it seems, to act contrary to this judgment *is* to act wrongly. The necessity appears to be merely logical. What more could be meant by the binding or necessitating force of the dictate of conscience?

The necessity involved is hypothetical, that which presupposes an end in view. "There is," Thomas writes, "also a conditioned necessity, that namely which is drawn from the supposition of some end; as someone may be under the necessity that, if he does not do this, he will not achieve his goal."[10] This is the only kind of necessity compatible with free will. The precept guiding and moving the will is a judgment that the good can be attained, or evil avoided, by such and such a kind of act. That is why no one can be bound by any precept save through the mediation of knowledge of the precept. (*Unde nullus ligatur per praeceptum aliquod nisi mediante scientia illius praecepti.*) An agent incapable of knowledge or simply ignorant of the precept cannot be bound by it. Furthermore, knowledge of the precept and the precept bind in mutually dependent ways; knowledge of the precept binds because the precept binds and the precept cannot bind unless it is known. But what makes the precept binding? "It is clear that conscience is said to bind by the power of the divine precept," Thomas said.[11]

The dictate of conscience borrows its force from the general principle it applies to these circumstances *hic et nunc.* That is why *synderesis* has to be presupposed to any discussion of conscience. It is because there are common principles of human action we cannot gainsay—expressing the end without which the human agent cannot be fulfilled and/or the means without which that end cannot be achieved—that a judgment of what is to be done here and now on penalty of eschewing the human good necessitates obedience. The principles of *synderesis*, natural law, are the first rule of human acts; conscience, presupposing them, is a measured measure, a derivative rule, but proximate.[12]

The notion of an erroneous conscience depends upon there being objective norms with reference to which a particular dictate is seen to be wrong. But, if this agent either does not know the general norm or does not see that his conscience is dictating an act which is in conflict with that norm, he is bound to act in accord with that judgment or dictate. But this, as we have seen, is not the end of the story. If an erroneous conscience binds, it does not excuse; that is, an erroneous dictate of conscience must be obeyed, but the obeying of it is morally wrong.

Now that seems to put the agent in an impossible position, one of *perplexitas*, as Thomas calls it, such that he necessarily must act badly. An erroneous conscience is an instance of ignorance, of not knowing the correct assessment of a proposed course of action. If the ignorance in which one acts is voluntary, then it does not excuse. An agent may choose not to inquire into the demands of justice, say, with the idea that the less he knows, the less constrained his actions will be. Here, ignorance is directly voluntary, chosen, willed. It may be indirectly voluntary if it is a matter of negligence, of one not putting his mind to know what he is held to know. Thomas sums up these two possibilities and says, "If then reason or conscience should err voluntarily, either directly or because of negligence, being in error about something one is held to know, then such error does not prevent the will which is in accord with erring reason or conscience from being evil."[13] Is such a person simply caught, unable to extricate himself from the dilemma of being bound to obey his conscience and thus bound to do wrong? Thomas suggests an analogy with the one whose motivation in acting is vainglory: whether or not he does what he ought to do, he does wrong. Is he thereby fated to do evil? No, Thomas says, because he can abandon his evil intention. "Similarly," he continues, "supposing error of reason or conscience which proceeds from a non-excusing ignorance, evil in the will necessarily follows. However, such a man is not *perplexus,* because he can correct his error, since his ignorance is both vincible and voluntary."[14] An act performed in invincible ignorance—an ignorance for which one can in no way be held accountable—would fail to qualify as a human act. Say I move my arm, the sun glances off the dial of my watch and blinds a person across the street, causing him to trip, fall from a window, crushing three pedestrians and fatally injuring himself, I being wholly unaware of this whole sequence. What did I do? Nothing. There is no human act involved of which those things I mentioned would be the component, descriptive notes. There is no point in asking in such a set of circumstances whether I acted well or badly. *Gaudium et Spes* maintains that it is not rare for conscience to err from invincible ignorance without losing its dignity ("*Non raro tamen evenit ex ignorantia invincibili conscientiam errare, quin inde suam dignitatem amittat.*" no. 16) This sentence is often cited as marking a great moral breakthrough that received concrete expression in *Dignitatis Humanae.*[15]

There is a curious piece on conscience by the late Karl Rahner to which Theo Belmens has recently drawn attention, and I note that Cardinal Ratzinger refers to this article of Belmens's in his address to the American bishops. I will not say he gives it his imprimatur, but he does not disagree with it. This article of Karl Rahner's bears superficial resemblances to traditional teaching on the matter. "Therefore a subjective judgment is a last court of appeal beyond which there can be no other. Objective norms have to be grasped as absolutely binding. That is why a dictate of conscience is absolutely binding for a decision of human freedom."[16] While allowing that not every opinion, preference, or prejudice can claim to be a dictate of conscience, Rahner adds that even a genuine dictate of conscience may be erroneous. It emerges, however, that he thinks erroneous conscience is a misnomer. Meanwhile, he has surprising things to say about the way conscience binds. This does not arise from the object of the act, which, whether erroneously or not, one judges to be here and now what he should do. "The absolute dignity and obligation of a dictate of conscience does not come properly and solely from the single categorical concrete value with which it is concerned. Why would a single human life, which is perishable after all, be able to demand for itself the absolute right to be respected?"[17]

Alluding to the hypothetical necessity of the judgment arrived at by conscience–"If one wishes to achieve a goal, one must use the necessary means to achieve it"–Rahner suggests that the end, too, is conditional. "Are health, peace, and some kind of happiness values that must be *unconditionally* achieved?" Nothing in the world of concrete realities and values, to which binding decisions of conscience refer, justifies such an absolute claim. If there are any absolute claims, they must come from elsewhere. And then he offers this startling conclusion.

> If there exists a more basic and general source of obligation, prior to individual values, we see right away that this source of absolute moral claims can be effective also in an erroneous conscience, one that errs about individual concrete realities, without erring about the foundation of their absolute claim. In other words: In both the right *and* the erroneous decisions of conscience, despite their disagreement about the concrete moral value, one and the same basic moral reality is at work. The error refers only to the concrete data, not to what bestows upon them their absolute obligation. That is why the concept of "erroneous conscience" is a misnomer. There are no truly erroneous dictates of conscience. If there were, they would not be dictates of conscience because they would not claim an absolute obligation.[18]

Chapter 2, section 3 of *Veritatis Splendor*, might be commenting on this very thing, which sounds very much like a dismissal of any distinction between the real and apparent good. The judgment of Theo Belmens on this article of Rahner's seems fully justified.[19]

Deliberation and Prospective Conscience

Although the judgment of conscience is often portrayed as the application of a general principle to particular circumstances (*applicatio notitiae ad actum*),[20] it is also linked to the role of *consilium* in seeking the appropriate means to the end.[21] Conscience is linked to counsel or *consilium* when it is prospective, concerned with what is to be done, not when it is retrospective, assessing what has been done.[22]

In Thomas's analysis of the human act, deliberation (*consilium*) precedes choice, since it is the inquiry into what precisely is to be chosen. "It is clear," he writes,

> that the act of reason directing things that are for the sake of the
> end and the act of the will under the command of reason tending
> to it are mutually ordered to one another. Hence, in the act of will
> that is choice something of reason appears, namely, order, and in
> deliberation, which is an act of reason, something of the will ap-
> pears as its matter, since deliberation is concerned with things a
> man wishes to do, and also as motive, since it is because a man
> wills the end that he is moved to deliberate about what is for the
> sake of the end. [23]

What Thomas has to say about deliberation complements what he
has to say about conscience. Thus the inquiry into what is to be done
here and now presupposes not only the deliverances of *synderesis*, viz.
natural law principles, but also wisdom and science, moral science.[24]
Natural law principles express the end to be pursued and those means
without which the end cannot be achieved, hence their necessity. But
practical reasoning also involves theoretical knowledge of ourselves
and the world as well as universal principles and precepts of action
short of necessary ones—most of them, we suppose, less than necessary rules for action.[25] We deliberate in the light of such principles
with an eye to judging what is to be done here and now.

When the relevance of the role of deliberation in the human act to
the understanding of conscience is accepted, a much discussed passage in *Quaestio Disputata de Veritate* becomes less troublesome. There,
Thomas is confronting an objection that equates conscience and free
will (*liberum arbitrium*): Conscience is a dictate of reason that is nothing other than a judgment, but judgment pertains to free judgment, as
the name suggests; therefore, it seems that conscience and free will
are identical.

In replying to this, Thomas notes that the judgment of conscience
and that of free will are both alike and unlike. They are alike in being
concerned with this particular act in the manner of appraisal (*in via
qua est examinans*). But the judgment of conscience, because it is purely
cognitive, differs from the judgment of free will, which is the application of knowledge to the affections, a judgment that is the judgment of
choice. This difference between them is the reason that, while the judgment of choice may be perverted, the judgment of conscience is not,
the latter being arrived at when one examines something imminently
to be done and judges it as though still reasoning from principles: this,

namely to fornicate with this woman, is evil. And that's the judgment of conscience in this passage. When he begins to act on it, however, many other circumstances, like the pleasure of fornication, rush in upon him, desire for which may so obstruct reason that its judgment, the judgment of conscience, is rejected, set aside, or ignored. Thus it is that one can err in choice and not in conscience—and we might say remorse presupposes that possibility; indeed, he acts contrary to conscience and is said to act with a bad conscience insofar as what he does is not in accord with the judgment of knowledge.[26]

The question has arisen as to whether Thomas really wishes to talk of rival judgments here rather than of the failure of a judgment of what ought to be done, the failure to influence the will's choice. Theo Belmens has made a strong case against interpreting Thomas as meaning two rival judgments in this passage. It is essential to see his reasons for this interpretation, however, because one can applaud the reasons without accepting his interpretation.[27] His concern is the view that there can be a rival particular judgment that overrides the particular judgment of conscience, the judgment of conscience that this act here and now falls under the universal prohibition of the kind of act it is. That is, given a correct dictate of conscience with respect to a singular deed to be done, there is still possible another correct, conflicting, and overriding judgment, the judgment of choice. That's what Belmens is worried about.

To say that one freely acts contrary to the judgment of conscience can mean several different things. If *conscience* is taken broadly to include natural law principles as well as what one holds on the basis of moral science *à la* Cardinal Ratzinger in *anamnesis*,[28] one could act contrary to a rule one accepts out of ignorance of the true circumstances. Thus, a person who accepts the prohibition of adultery might, out of ignorance of the circumstances—for example, mistaking another woman for one's wife (this is Thomas's example)—unwittingly act contrary to the principle he accepts. But clearly such a case does not entail that adultery is sometimes morally permissible.

If *conscience* is taken, however, in the narrow sense of the here and now dictate that this act is now obligatory, freely to act to the contrary can only be due to weakness. To choose to act contrary to the principle conscience has applied to these circumstances is implicitly to bring the choice under a contrary principle. If that contrary principle were enunciated, it would express a falsehood, not another and contrary morally permissible mode of conduct. I think that answers Belmens's concern. To suggest anything else is to hold that contraries can be simultaneously true. Choice may override the judgment of conscience, but it cannot do this in a morally defensible way. Belmens rightly opposes those who suggest that there is some private moral code at the existential singular level that overrides conscience and the principles it applies. The singular must instantiate some stateable principle. When stated, that principle will be seen to conflict with the true principle.

Such fanciful possibilities have usually (if not always) been advanced in discussions of sexual morality to provide a basis for licitly acting contrary to prohibitions of adultery, masturbation, homosexuality, and so forth. Of course it will not do to say, "My conscience tells me contraception is permitted." "Conscience" would have to be taken here in the broad sense, such that conscience bears on general claims for licit moral behavior. The discussion could then proceed in a variety of ways. A Catholic who understands (a) what the church teaches on the matter and (b) the binding character of that teaching, can scarcely claim that his inability to understand arguments against contraception makes the prohibition inoperative in his case. Of course, to accept the prohibition is to accept its reasonableness, and a human agent, on whom it is incumbent to act according to reason, would want to go beyond the considerations just given to understand the philosophical arguments presupposed by *Humanae Vitae*.

Belmens is right to reject the suggestion that there is a defensible morality different from that based on divine and natural law.

On Toasting Conscience and the Pope

Cardinal Newman has often been invoked by dissident theologians in the wake of Vatican II. The great English convert's *On Consulting the Faithful in Matters of Doctrine*, for example, has been taken to be a defense of a populist church in which the dicta of bishops and pope can be overridden by the practices of the faithful. This is hardly the usual understanding of the *sensus fidelium*, as it functioned, for example, in the Bull of the Assumption–and clearly, I think, not at all what Newman meant. "A physician may consult the pulse of his patient," he wrote, "but not in the same sense that the patient consults him."[29] So too Newman's *A Letter to the Duke of Norfolk* has been used as precedent for the view that the thoughtful Catholic may conscientiously disagree with papal teaching. Everyone knows at least these lines from the letter: "I add one remark," Newman writes. "Certainly, if I am obliged to bring religion into after-dinner toasts (which indeed does not seem quite the thing) I shall drink–to the Pope, if you please–still, to Conscience first, and to the Pope afterwards." This has been taken to mean that, while one might listen to what *Humanae Vitae* has to say about contraception, one can legitimately and conscientiously override its prohibition. But what does Newman say?

He means by *conscience* what Thomas means when he contrasts it with *synderesis*; for Newman, conscience is a particular dictate bearing immediately on what is to be done. That is why, he writes, "it cannot come into direct collision with the Church's or the Pope's infallibility; which is engaged on general propositions, and in the condemnation of particular and given errors."[30] Newman seems to have in mind the pope's directives as civil ruler, perhaps the traffic laws of Vatican City, though he also mentions the disagreement of Peter with Paul at Antioch and Liberius's excommunication of Athanasius. Presumably he means that Paul was within his rights in arguing against Peter and that Athanasius could be confident that his actions were not deserving of excommunication. There seems no way in the world in which the dissenting moral theologian can take comfort from what Newman says.

Thomas actually makes a similar point.

> A spiritual bond is stronger than a bodily one, and an intrinsic one stronger than an extrinsic. But conscience is an intrinsic spiritual bond, whereas the prelate is an extrinsic one, as it seems, since every prelate operates through a temporal dispensation, which at the advent of eternity is dissolved, as the Gloss notes in 1 Corinthians 15:24. It seems therefore that conscience rather than a prelate should be obeyed.[31]

The reason for this is that conscience derives its binding power from either the divine precept or from natural law; therefore, to compare the way conscience and a command of the prelate bind is to compare the way the divine command and the prelate's command bind. Whenever the command of the prelate conflicts with conscience, then conscience is to be obeyed, since this is simply to recognize that God's command takes precedence over that of the prelate when they conflict.

Having said this, however, Thomas observes that the situation varies depending on whether conscience is correct or erroneous. The correct conscience simply and perfectly takes precedence over that of the prelate; *simply*, because its obligation cannot be taken away or set aside without committing sin; *perfectly*, because a correct conscience not only binds in such a way that to follow it is to avoid falling into sin, but it also makes the one following it rather than the prelate's contrary command immune from sin.

It is otherwise with an erroneous conscience. It binds as over against the command of the prelate in indifferent matter only in a given respect (*secundum quid*) and imperfectly. *Secundum quid*, because it does not oblige always, but only so long as it endures: one can and one ought to alter such a conscience. *Imperfectly*, because it binds in such a way that one who follows it does not incur sin, but not in such a way that the one following it avoids sin when there is a contrary command of the prelate in such indifferent matter. This gets fairly *recherché* here. In such a case one sins, whether he does not act, because then he acts contrary to conscience, or whether he acts, because then he disobeys the prelate. It would be a greater sin if he did not do what conscience dictates while conscience remains unchanged, since it binds more than the command of the prelate.

St. Thomas would, on the basis of that passage I've gone into more at length, thus agree with the order of precedence in Newman's toasts: first to conscience, then to the pope, since this means, God first, then the pope. And, when pope and church teach infallibly, to toast them is to toast God, no conflict being possible. That is what infallibility means.

Notes

1. *Nicomachean Ethics* VII, 2, 1146a28. Aristotle also invokes a literary example. "And if moral weakness makes a man abandon any and every opinion, moral weakness will occasionally be morally good, as, for example, in

the case of Neoptolemus in Sophocles's *Philoctetes.* Neoptolemus deserves praise when he does not abide by the resolution which Odysseus had persuaded him to adopt, because it gives him pain to tell a lie." (1146a18ff.)

2. It has sometimes been argued that Aristotle–and derivatively Thomas Aquinas–has two different accounts of practical reasoning between which he vacillates: first, the rule/application model, and, second, the end/means model. In the latter understanding of practical reasoning, we begin with a goal or end and then seek appropriate means to attain the end. Since principles express the end, the major premise of the practical syllogism may be said to contain the end, and the minor premise the judgment of how the end can best be achieved. The two models, sometimes thought to be opposed, can thus be seen to stress two aspects of the same kind of discourse.

3. *Nicomachean Ethics,* 1105b12-18; see Thomas, Lecture IV, n. 288.

4. Thomas learned this parallel between the speculative and practical uses of our mind from Aristotle, and it became a constant of his treatment of the first principles of practical reasoning. "*Unde et in natura humana, in quantum attingit angelicam, oportet esse cognitionem veritatis* sine inquisitione et *in* speculativis *et in* practicis; *et hanc quidem cognitionem oportet esse principium totius cognitionis sequentis, sive speculativae sive practicae, cum principia oportet esse stabiliora et certiora. Unde et hanc cognitionem oportet homini naturaliter inesse . . . Oportet etiam hanc cognitionem* habitualem *esse, ut in promptu existat ea uti cum fuerit necesse. Sicut autem animae humanae est quidam habitus naturalis quo principia speculativarum scientiarum cognoscit, quem vocamus*intellectum principiorum*; ita in ipsa est quidam habitus naturalis primorum principiorum operabilium, quae sunt naturalia principia iuris naturalis; qui quidem habitus ad*synderesim *pertinet.*" *Q. D. de Veritate,* q. 17, a. 1, c.; cf. *Summa Theologiae,* Ia-IIae, q. 94, a. 2, c.

5. Thomas gives two examples, in response to the objection that *synderesis* applies only to the *ratio superior,* one natural law principle which is of superior reason (*Deo esse obediendum*), another which pertains to the *ratio inferior.* One ought to live according to reason (*secundum rationem esse vivendum*). *Q. D. de Veritate,* q. 16, a. 1, ad 9m.

6. Thomas will thus distinguish two senses of reason or *ratio: ratio ut natura* and *ratio ut ratio.* It is proper to reason to put things together, to move from one truth to another, to engage in discourse. But taken as nature, there are things reason knows right off, *statim,* without discourse. Cf. *Q. D. de Veritate,* q. 17, a. 1, c.

7. The work of my colleague Alasdair MacIntyre, from *After Virtue* a decade ago and continuing through a series of books of fundamental importance, culminating in his Gifford lectures, *Three Rival Forms of Ethical Inquiry,* stresses the dialectical difficulty of arguing that such common principles are embedded in quite different ethical traditions. The point is that they are always *embedded* in quite concrete, and differing, traditions. As elicited and articulated in relative independence of this tradition or that, they have an abstract and unfamiliar air. That is not how they are learned. Of course, not all traditions are legitimately different ways of embodying these principles and

they become, when made explicit, the means of criticizing the tradition. Cardinal Ratzinger uses *anamnesis* as a synonym for *synderesis*. The common principles invite what Edmund Wilson called, in another connection, the "shock of recognition." Sometimes the shock is felt more than the recognition.

8. " . . . *dicendum quod iudicium est duplex: in universali, et hoc pertinet ad synderesim; et* in particulari *operabili, et hoc est iudium electionis, et hoc pertinet ad liberum arbitrium.*" *Q. D. de Veritate,* a. 1, ad 15m.

9. The contrast is first made in q. 16, a. 2, ad 1m, and then becomes thematic in q. 17 of the *De Veritate.*

10. "*Alia vero est necessitas conditionata, scilicet ex finis suppositione; sicut imponitur alicui necessitas ut si non fecerit hoc, non consequitur suum praemium.*" *Q. D. de Veritate,* q. 17, a. 3, c.

11. "*Unde cum conscientia nihil aliud sit quam applicatio notitiae ad actum, constat quod conscientia ligare dicitur vi praecepti divini.*" This and the preceding quotation are also taken from *Q. D. de Veritate,* q. 17, a. 3, c.

12. " . . . *conscientia non est prima regula humanorum operum, sed magis synderesis; conscientia autem est quasi regula regulata; unde nihil mirum, si error in ea potest accidere.*" *Q. D. de Veritate,* q. 17, a. 2, ad 7m.

13. "*Si igitur ratio vel conscientia erret errore voluntario, vel directe, vel propter negligentiam, quia est error circa id quod quis scire tenetur; tunc talis error rationis vel conscientiae non excusat quin voluntas concordans rationi vel conscientiae sic erranti, sit mala.*" *IaIIae,* q. 19, a. 6. c.

14. "*Et similiter, supposito errore rationis vel conscientiae qui procedit ex ignorantia non excusante, necesse est quod sequatur malum in voluntate. Nec tamen est homo perplexus: quia potest ab errore recedere, cum ignorantia sit vincibilis et voluntaria.*" *IaIIae,* q. 19, a. 6, ad 3m.

15. This is almost to suggest that the point of *Dignitatis Humanae* was to celebrate the lamentable fact that so many have not yet embraced the true faith. Freedom of conscience in matters of religion has been invoked to suggest a relativism or indifferentism. In this regard, the contemporary reflections of Guy de Broglie, S.J., are worth rereading: *Le Droit Naturel à la Liberté Religieuse* (Paris: Beauchesne, 1964).

16. Karl Rahner, "Conscience," in *Theological Investigations* 22, trans. Joseph Donceel, S.J. (New York: Crossroad, 1990), pp. 3-13.

17. Ibid., p. 8.

18. Ibid.

19. Cf. Theo Belmens, "Le Paradoxe de la Conscience Erronée d'Abélard à Karl Rahner," *Revue Thomiste* (1990), pp. 570-586, esp. pp. 582ff.

20. *Q. D. de Veritate,* q. 17, a. 1, c. *in fine.*

21. "*Illa enim via qua per scientiam inspicimus quid agendum est, quasi consiliantes, est similis inventioni, per quam ex principiis investigamus conclusiones.*" *Q. D. de Veritate,* q. 17, a. 1, c.

22. The appraisal of this act as right or wrong is twofold. "*Una secundum quod per habitum scientiae dirigimur in aliquid faciendum vel non faciendum. Alio*

modo secundum quod actus postquam factus est, examinatur ad habitum scientiae, an sit rectus vel non rectus." Q. D. de Veritate, q. 17, a. 1, c.

23. *IaIIae,* q. 14, a. 1, ad 1m.

24. *Q. D. de Veritate,* q. 17, a. 1.

25. *IaIIae,* q. 14, a. 6, c. is an interesting text in this regard, The proper starting point of deliberation is the end, the human good, which is presupposed, but there are also principles or starting points drawn from sense perception, e.g. this is bread or iron, and whatever else of a general sort drawn from speculative or practical science that is relevant, e.g., that adultery is prohibited by God and that a man cannot live without proper nourishment. One does not deliberate or take counsel of such matters but assumes them. The whole inquiry terminates in something that it is in our power to do now. "*Terminus autem inquisitionis est id quod statim est in potestate nostra ut faciamus."*

26. "*. . . dicendum quod iudicium conscientiae et liberi arbitrii quantum ad aliquid differunt, et quantum ad aliquid conveniunt. Conveniunt enim quantum ad hoc quod utrumque est de hoc particulari actu; competit autem iudicium conscientiae in via qua est examinans; et in hoc differt iudicium utriusque a iudiciio synderesis et differunt iudicium conscientiae et liberi arbitrii, quia iudicium conscientiae consistit in pura cognitione, iudicium autem liberi arbitrii in applicatione cognitionis ad affectionem: quod quidem iudicium est iudicium electionis. Et ideo contingit quandoque quod iudicium liberi arbitrii pervertitur, non autem conscientiae; sicut cum aliquis examinat aliquid quod imminet faciendum, et iudicat, quasi adhuc speculando per principia, hoc esse malum, utpote fornicari cum hac muliere; sed quantum incipit applicare ad agendum, occurrunt undique multae circumstantiae ad ipsum actum, utpote fornicationis delectatio, ex cuius concupiscentiae ligatur ratio, ne eius dictamen in eius reiectionem prorumpat. Et sic aliquis errat in eligendo, et non in conscientia; sed contra conscientiam facit, in quantum factum iudicio scientiae non concordat."* Q. D. de Veritate, q. 17, a. 1, ad 4m.

27. I must confess to being unconvinced by Father Belmens's response to my "The Right Deed for the Wrong Reason" (*Doctor Communis* 43 [1990], pp. 234-249 [reprinted in my *Aquinas on Human Action: A Theory of Practice,* Washington: Catholic University of America Press, 1992, pp. 220-239]). Father Belmens's response, "Le 'jugement prudentiel' chez saint Thomas: Réponse à R. McInerny," is found in *Revue thomiste* (1991), pp. 414-420. Father Belmens insists that *iudicium* in *iudicium electionis* cannot mean what it means in *iudicium conscientiae.* Thus, when a person, under the impulse of passion, chooses to act contrary to his conscience, the act of his will is not to be taken as an instance of rational appetite, that is, as following on cognition. I take this to be a denial of what Thomas means by will. The man who correctly judges that an act of sexual congress with this woman would be adulterous, and nevertheless engages in that act, chooses to do so—otherwise it is not a human act and neither good nor bad. If it is a choice, it is the execution of some judgment. In discussions of weakness of will, both Aristotle and Thomas speak of practical syllogism and say that the man who acts contrary to his conscience chooses under another judgment he doubtless would be ashamed to articulate, viz. never

pass up an opportunity for venereal pleasure. But of course he need not enunciate the judgment of conscience or the precept which it applies. To say that the reasoning of the weak man is not reasoning but the corruption of reasoning should be taken to mean not that it is no reasoning at all, but that it is bad reasoning. In the same way, when bad actions are said to fall away from intellect and reason (*deficimus ab intellectu et ratione*), this cannot be taken to mean they are not human acts, that is, proceeding from reason and will. Even bad human acts are human acts. Father Belmens seems to me to attribute to the act of will in the choice of the weak man what is appropriate to the impulse of passion, which leads to the judgment opposed to that of conscience, which choice perversely follows. I fear that my difference with Father Belmens concerns choice as an act of will rather than *iudicium* as such. Thomas likes to recall Aristotle's hesitation about choice. Is it an *appetitivus intellectus* or an *appetitus intellectivus*? Father Belmens appears to want choice to be a movement of will unspecified by any judgment.

28. See Cardinal Ratzinger's discussion, pages 12ff., above.

29. Cf. Ian Ker, *John Henry Newman* (Oxford: Oxford University Press, 1988), p. 480ff.

30. See Ker's discussion, ibid., pp. 688ff.

31. *Q. D. de Veritate*, q. 17, a. 5, *sed contra.*

6

Conscience and Responsibility in Christian Ethics

ROBERT SPAEMANN

The word *responsibility* is in vogue, and it has become common practice to describe moral behavior as "responsible" behavior. Max Weber made the distinction between "the ethics of conviction" and the "ethics of responsibility" where both moral attitudes were still considered as genuine alternatives.[1] However, Weber was of the opinion that, in order to be consistent, following the ethics of conviction meant abstaining from politics, and a politician should act according to the ethics of responsibility. Today's thinking has thrust great emphasis upon the ethics of responsibility, which seems to have become synonymous with morality; even Christian moral teaching is largely being formulated in terms of what is understood to be a person's responsibility. For Max Weber, "responsibility" was directly opposed to "conviction." Conviction is still often considered as synonymous with conscience. A delinquent by conviction is also called a conscientious offender, and conscientious objections are still accepted by the state as a reason for refusing to do military service. In contemporary discussions on moral theology, the concepts of responsibility and conscience are being closely pushed together. Both serve the same purpose in decisions where discretion is called for, as opposed to so-called legal ethics or ethics of duty. In this context, responsibility means acting according to how our conscience guides us and making a purely objective, discretionary decision.

The following text will first of all examine the reasons behind the current predominance of this theme. Then we shall ask how feasible it is to adopt responsibility as a basic moral concept and what it can achieve in interpreting our fundamental moral intuitions and defining the boundary lines of human responsibility. Finally, we must ask what are the specific Christian motives in considering responsibility—motives which, in this so-called age of responsibility, make it important to distinguish "Christian ethics of responsibility."

The Usefulness and Limits of the Concept of Responsibility

The term *ethics of responsibility* has the peculiarity of creating a moral, social, and legal framework for all our moral decisions, namely, that of responsibility. What we consider to be our responsibility can be shown clearly in this example from everyday life: A doctor gives me an injection and prescribes some medicine, telling me to take ten drops three times a day. I follow his instructions. The doctor is responsible for prescribing the right medicine and the correct dosage. I leave this to him because of his specific expertise in judging the chemical effects and the resulting organic changes. Nevertheless, the doctor's responsibility is limited in several respects. For example, he must be able to rely on the fact that the medicine package really does contain what is stated on the label and that the nurse hands him the correct syringe. He is not normally responsible for mistakes in such areas, any more than he is for the wider consequences when his treatment succeeds and its effect on third parties. For example, a doctor cannot be deemed responsible for successfully treating and discharging an abusive father when his wife and family would much rather see him dead and buried—even when the patient then proceeds to destroy his family. Were a doctor to extend the limits of his responsibility to include such broader consequences and adapt his code of practice accordingly, he would breach his medical code of ethics, and we would have reason not to trust him. If he does take on such a responsibility and concerns himself with the broader actions of his patient beyond his medical condition, he may only do so when he has fulfilled his specific responsibility as a doctor.

Responsibility always exists for something or to someone. For the doctor, this someone is primarily the patient, who sees the doctor as responsible for his health. Second, in certain circumstances, the doctor also has a responsibility to the health insurance companies insofar as they bear the financial cost of the treatment.

For the nurse who prepares the syringe, the sphere of responsibility is narrower: normally, she just has to follow the doctor's instructions. Her duty to be conscientious can also be described as a responsibility; however, this is better referred to as professional ethics. This nurse may have certain responsibilities for storing the medical supplies so as to avoid mixing them up. She would take over responsibility whenever the doctor was not present, or when he gave her instructions that were obviously based on misinformation or malicious intent. In such a situation, it is her specific responsibility not to follow instructions, but rather to notify the doctor, in cases of misinformation, or, where malicious intent is involved, to appeal to a higher authority or warn the patient. Although the nurse takes over responsibility in such exceptional cases, it is not her duty to check constantly the validity of the doctor's instructions. If subordinates were always expected to carry out such checks, the system of issuing and carrying out orders could never work–either in the professional or political sphere. The human community simply cannot function without so-called preconceptions. One must be able to assume that orders are lawful and correct (which is, of course, refutable), and that they only need to be checked and corrected in certain, special cases.

What can be learned from this example? There is no question of responsibility when precise instructions are given and followed. However, when someone has to organize the administration of a specific and complex area or is responsible for carrying out a complex task, relying on his own expertise to make a range of judgments, and when that person is legally responsible for the results of his actions, then political responsibility extends further than purely moral responsibility. Whoever has no luck in politics must go, and the man in charge is responsible for his subordinates' mistakes (and their consequences), even when, from a moral point of view, the mistake is not his fault. In most cases he selected the subordinates and therefore must accept responsibility for the tasks delegated to them. Political, legal, and moral responsibility, therefore, do not necessarily overlap. Political responsibility is the broadest, legal responsibility the narrowest, and moral responsibility the most difficult to define clearly.

Four major factors have contributed to the increasing moral significance of the principle of responsibility[2] in our society:

1. the increasing complexity of daily life;
2. the identification of various social sub-systems;
3. the increasing ability of science to forecast the long-term, cumulative effects of human activity, and finally,
4. the rapid changes in the outside forces affecting human behavior.[3]

The Increasing Complexity of Daily Life

The increasing complexity of daily life is leading to a situation where correct action requires being able to make judgments in an ever-broader area. Carrying out a task correctly presupposes that the agent is not only employed as a means to an end but is himself informed of the overall objectives and has the necessary skill to carry them out. For example, if drilling exercises have been reduced in the army, this is because modern warfare no longer needs men who carry out their duty automatically, like cogs in a finely-tuned machine, but soldiers capable of thinking for themselves and completing their tasks independently. In complex situations one must be able to adapt, and only someone with the necessary skills can do this. Of course, for a large part of today's population, responsibility is continually being reduced. The lady from the cleaning company who cleans our offices no longer has the same level of responsibility as her predecessor. She simply follows instructions; to try to formulate a professional code of behavior in terms of her responsibilities would be purely cynical.

The Identification of Various Social Sub-systems

The differentiation of various social sub-systems has resulted in more and more people having several roles to play. These roles dictate certain patterns of behavior; however, coordinating these different roles requires making further spontaneous decisions that do not fall within any of these behavioral patterns. For example, in a democratic government an official has laws and regulations to follow. At the same time, as a citizen, he is also responsible for any eventual change in these laws.

Forecasting the Effects of Human Activity

Modern technology has rendered human activity extraordinarily effective. Nature is the reservoir of all our natural resources and at the same time the rubbish dump for all the waste created by our lifestyles, but it can no longer continually absorb the effects of human activity and restore the balance of nature. Furthermore, science shows us in ever-greater detail the cumulative effects of human activity. We have more smog alarms nowadays than before, simply because we are better able to take the necessary measurements. Before, nobody had even noticed the hole in the ozone layer, whereas now we not only know of its existence, but we have well-founded theories about its relationship to the use of chloro-fluorocarbons.

"It's none of my business" goes the old saying, but now the broader range of our activities combined with our increased knowledge of the consequences thereof have given us new areas of responsibility for which earlier generations could not be held accountable, such as the preservation of Earth's biosphere.

Rapid Change

With the ever-increasing rate of change in our way of life, it is difficult to rely on any definite and unchanging patterns of behavior—either in regard to oneself, or to others. Goethe's maxim "Do what is right in your own affairs, and the rest will take care of itself"[4] presupposes an unchanging social system where behavioral expectations are reciprocated. But what is "right in your own affairs" when you're a soldier dealing with modern means of mass destruction or a doctor who has to reckon with the possibilities of test-tube reproduction, genetic manipulation, organ transplants, and prolonging human life beyond any humane considerations? The traditional code of conduct for a soldier or a doctor does not give sufficient guidelines to deal with these situations in advance. Another point to be considered is that, for our forebears, the proven rule was "When in doubt, don't do anything which might prove to be wrong." The thinking behind this came from the belief that the world was a stable cosmos capable of maintaining its equilibrium regardless of our actions—whether we acted in one way, or another, or not at all.[5] Someone who does not vote in an election is not morally excused; he votes, as the saying goes, for the winning party. For every wrong action, there is a worse alternative, and apparently no action can be considered wrong in all circumstances, but in certain situations it will be the least wrong of two bad alternatives, that is, not doing anything will bring about worse results than actually doing something.

One could probably add further factors to those mentioned, but their combined effect has been to turn the specific moral phenomenon of responsibility into a model for interpreting morality in general. This exclusive focusing of ethics around the concept of responsibility has been influenced, of course, by certain elements of bourgeois ideology. Working-class professional ethics are totally ignored, and this also includes those who have not attended Catholic higher education institutes, for example.

The Christian Understanding of Responsibility

Can Christian ethical understanding also be interpreted according to certain categories of responsibility? First of all, it must be said that Christian ethics are not special ethics just for Christians, but for all people, because only Christian ethics can convey the real motives behind our actions. Similarly, the gospel and its application to our lives through the teachings of the church are correctives to the manmade moral guidelines that nonbelievers fall into. During his three-year ministry Jesus predominantly taught us about moral behavior, and it would be strange, therefore, if the church (of whom Jesus said, "Anyone who listens to you, listens to me" [Luke 10:16]) he taught and that continues to apply Christ's teachings had no competence or authority to teach in precisely this area of moral behavior. In regard to the moral guidelines of any age, the church has applied the teaching of St. Paul: "Test everything, hold on to what is good" (1 Thessalonians 5:21).

What are the criteria for this testing? They cannot be criteria foreign or extraneous to our own basic moral instincts with the result that these instincts would have to be disregarded in light of the teaching of gospel and the church. Rather, it is just the reverse: the gospel highlights these intuitions, purifies them, and frees them from corruption and false interpretation. It is our own human interests, desire for self-reliance, and human reasoning that encourage such false interpretation. Kant spoke of a "natural dialectic," a tendency to rationalize against any strict laws of duty.[6]

The gospel, which the church teaches, guides us and shows us how our consciences can be confused and manipulated by our own wishes, interests, preferences, likings, opinions and theories. All sorts of things can be concealed by the term *conscience*. Christ himself tells us this is possible: "The hour is coming when whoever kills you will think he is offering service to God" (John 16:2). Christ was no more inclined to teach us simply to follow our conscience than was Socrates. Rather, Jesus guides our conscience so that when we follow it, we don't automatically do wrong.

The idea of moral behavior as an awareness of one's responsibility doubtless has deep biblical roots. In scripture, the first reference made to the theme of morals is in the story of Cain and Abel. It is interesting in the light of our present discussion to look at how God questions Cain about the murder of his brother. God does not ask whether he has broken any law, but simply asks, "Where is your brother?" (Genesis 4:9). Significantly, Cain does not answer by denying a crime with which he has not yet been charged; rather, he passes back the responsibility: "Am I my brother's keeper?" meaning, "Am I supposed to know where he is?" Moral responsibility is described here in two ways: responsibility *for* someone, and second, accountability *to* someone. Cain is responsible for his brother. His brother has been entrusted to him; not only may he not kill him, but he is required to know where Abel is to be found. His responsibility *for* his brother is not the same as his primary accountability for his brother. One can dispose of one's responsibility for a human being by killing him. But, as the passage tells us, Abel's blood cries out to God. The murder does not remove accountability because this accountability cannot be removed. And that which cannot be removed is what we call God. The phrase "My brother's keeper" is the keyword for the Christian ethics of responsibility.

The New Testament often presents the Christian life as one of independent stewardship where one is answerable to someone. This is so in the parable of the unjust steward (Luke 16:1ff.) and in the parable of the talents, where the property-owner demands in return more than the original sum invested (Luke 19:11ff.); or in the story of the good Samaritan, who sees the need of his fellow traveler and straightaway assumes responsibility for him, from the time he lifts him up to the time when he offers to cover the costs at the inn where he lodges him (Luke 10:30ff.). To me, the focal point for any reflection about individual responsibility rests on what Jesus says in the gospel of John: "I no longer call you servants but friends, since a servant does not know his master's business" (John 15:15). When this is considered in the light of Jesus's summing up of the law by the command to love God and one's neighbor, then the verse in John may be interpreted thus: The servant performs orders without understanding their meaning or purpose. Therefore he has no possibility of variation or scope for decision. The friend, however, understands the intention of his master and thus he can act responsibly. When he has made God's love his own, he has the authority to act creatively. His actions are no longer inconsistent as he pursues self-interest, on the one hand, while trying to live within the constraints of respecting the law and carrying out his duties, on the other–duties that naturally curtail the pursuit of self-interest. Behavior is motivated much more by a single source: Love. Of course, we are a long way from such inner unity, such single-mindedness, for it is an ideal. It is the goal described by Christ when he says, "Be perfect as your Father in heaven is perfect" (Matthew 5:48). The Christian life is the Way to this goal, the Way is called Christ, and traveling along this Way is following him.

The essence of Christian ethics is not based on a code of legal rules but rather the positive awareness of a responsibility for those things protected by law and entrusted to men. This responsibility is above all an active responsibility for one another. To take an example from recent history: most Germans say, presumably with some truth, that they did not know what was happening to the Jews. But, for Christians, this in itself is an admission of guilt, for should they not have asked, after the Jews' deportation, "Where is my brother?" I say this with a certain reticence, because it is always easier to put down other Christians under the pretense of Christian self-criticism, especially when referring to those who lived before our time. I chose this example simply because, with the passage of time, it now serves as a good illustration to us all.

Understanding Ethical Intuition in Terms of Responsibility

We should now look at how to understand ethical intuition in terms of responsibility. What are the false interpretations not immediately visible, and what specific changes does the Christian faith make to the ethics of responsibility approach? In connection with this, it is useful to recall how Max Weber introduced the concept of an ethics of responsibility. Weber was pursuing a political rather than a general argument. He wanted to prove that those who held a radically pacifist position had no right to engage in politics due to their unconditional moral conviction that the use of weapons should be rejected. Weber had great respect for those who would not kill under any circumstances. He did not believe in any way that a person of such moral conviction should be held responsible for the fateful consequences of his abstention. It may well be that widespread pacifism within a political party could encourage the outbreak of war. According to Weber, if an individual is convinced that he must not bear arms, he is not obliged to review his position in the light of such consequences. However, if a pacifist becomes politically active and starts a movement encouraging popular refusal to bear arms, he can be held accountable for the consequences. According to Weber, if a politician is to act in a morally responsible way, he must consider his actions in terms of their consequences and the effect they will have on the community as a whole. To this end, he must consider the pros and cons of all possible courses of action open to him. If, for moral reasons, a particular course of action is not open to him, then, in certain circumstances, he must surrender his responsibility. Weber believed that no rational criteria existed for choosing between these two positions. He also believed that the ethics of responsibility included a willingness to admit guilt for one's responsibilities and that, for this reason, saints had to be moralists of conviction.

Proponents of Christian ethics and those in favor of ethics based purely on reason–and Christian ethics are based on reason–would object to this point of view. For when one can make an arbitrary choice between the two positions, then neither deserves to be called ethical. If I consider an action to be good purely based on my own moral standards, the words *good* and *bad* lose their meaning. Either these words mean "right or wrong according to an absolute standard," or they have no meaning at all. Furthermore, the idea that someone should become guilty because of the responsibility he bears is a lapse into polytheism: offending one deity to please another. Of course, it happens all the time that certain values and good deeds have to suffer so that others may be justified instead. This can be justified or unjustified. Christ tells us, "If your right eye causes you to sin, pluck it out and throw it away; it is better that you lose one of your members than that your whole body be thrown into hell" (Matthew 5:29). When the authority to which responsibility is due is the one, true God and not our own idols and values, and when the level of our responsibility is based on reasonableness, then we can never consider it our duty to feel morally guilty.

We can certainly assume from this that only the concept of finite responsibility can have any meaning for us, and that our responsibility is never of an infinite nature. And so, in political situations, it makes sense to distinguish between ethics of conviction and ethics of responsibility, but is not otherwise considered a worthwhile exercise, in particular, because those whom Weber considers proponents of responsibility-ethics would consider themselves as following their moral convictions. The pacifist claims that, if only a sufficient majority followed him, there would be no wars. But someone has to make a start in order to build up this following. Even terrorists present themselves in court as people driven by their moral convictions, acting in the belief that they are fulfilling their responsibility to ensure the best destiny for mankind, a belief that excuses them from observing normal human rights and civic duties.

As a rule, philosophical discussions usually talk about an antithesis, related to Weber's but more detailed, that is, teleological and deontological ethics. So-called teleological ethics are also known as consequentialism or utilitarianism, meaning that the moral quality of an action or omission is determined by the entirety of the consequences of this action or omission, compared to that of every possible alternative action or omission. Deontological ethics makes a limit to this calculation whereby certain types of behavior will always be rejected, regardless of their consequences, for example, the deliberate, direct killing of an innocent individual, torture, or extramarital sexual relations. However, it must be made clear that there can be no *purely* deontological ethic; that is, one which ignores all the consequences of a given action. (On the other hand, purely consequentialist ethics can be upheld in theory but do not work in practice for reasons of principle.) It is impossible to ignore all the consequences of an action, because the very nature of an action is for it to have an effect. Thus, an action that ignores all its consequences cannot really be called an action at all.

In view of this, the question remains: For which consequences are we responsible, beyond the intended direct effects of the action? Consequentialists will argue: all consequences. However, there is a difference of opinion over the criteria for evaluation. Classical utilitarianism has a simple parameter for this: the greatest possible happiness for the greatest possible number, happiness here defined more precisely as pleasure or actual subjective well-being. Other positions try to differentiate moral standards. They agree only that a particular action cannot be called good or bad in itself, but rather its quality is determined by an overall evaluation of its consequences. As we have already noted, this procedure breaks down for a number of reasons. For one thing, it is usually not feasible to carry out such a long-term, overall estimation or a true evaluation of the consequences. Furthermore, such a thought process would make any kind of action impossible. Action in this case is made distinct from the natural course of events in that the protagonist can specify certain consequences of his action that differ from what normally would have occurred. These specific consequences are called *purposes*. In relation to these purposes, all other consequences are relegated in their importance to being *side effects*. But if we are equally responsible for all the consequences of our actions, it would become impossible to rank the consequences, set a goal, and undertake a finite action. In fact, consequentialism puts man in the place of God, who is present in all things, even a sparrow falling from a roof or a hair from a head. When there is no distinction between purpose and side effect, then there is no requirement for finite action.[7]

If the consequentialist interpretation of the ethics of responsibility were acceptable, then we could only have one, single aim: to make the world better. Whoever had this goal would be allowed to do anything to achieve it, because all means would be permissible. St. Paul's exhortation not to do evil that good may result (Romans 3:8) would serve no purpose. For nothing could be considered evil when it produces something good, at least not when the good is intended.

Another, more important objection to this understanding of the ethics of responsibility is that it is counterproductive. The state of the world would decline if everyone felt entitled to do all he thought suitable to improve it. Finally, the consequentialist ethical view would mean abandoning independent moral judgments in favor of experts and futurologists. Only experts can tell us the foreseeable long-term results of our actions. The National Socialists believed that the liquidation of the Jews would be of great benefit to the whole of mankind. The Westphalian peasant farmers who hid Jews did not do so because they could disprove this theory, but because it was totally irrelevant for them. They knew in their conscience what they had learnt in catechism, that innocent people must not be killed. Consequentialism, on the contrary, devalues the moral intuitions of simple people, leaving it all in the hands of so-called experts.[8]

As previously stated, deontological ethics also cannot truly exist in its pure form. No one could really conceive of defining morality as a series of rules that were always valid, regardless of the circumstances. Certain actions can be considered good in their nature and type. But to be good in a concrete situation, they must also fit with the time, place, and circumstances. When first aid is needed to save someone's life, then saying the rosary instead would be a bad thing to do, although praying the rosary is no doubt a good thing to do in itself. Curiously, a certain asymmetry comes into play here. No action can be considered always appropriate, regardless of the circumstances. We take responsibility for all our good actions, but taking this responsibility means we must make a reasonable assessment of the situation. On the other hand, there are actions that are intrinsically bad, where no attention is paid to the surrounding circumstances. More precisely, such an action would mean having to violate a basic responsibility we have toward ourselves or to our neighbors. This asymmetry is expressed in a saying of Dionysius the Areopagite, quoted some fifty times by Thomas Aquinas in his text on moral theories: "*Bonum ex integra causa, malum ex quocumque defectu.*"[9] This means that for something to be good, it must be completely good; any single fault can make it bad, for example, the wrong place, the wrong time, or even a wrong motive pursued through an action that is good in itself. Conversely, a good motive cannot reprieve a bad action.

This asymmetrical relationship would be meaningless if we were all responsible at all times for making the world a better place to live in, and all other responsibilities became subordinate to this overall responsibility. As proved, however, this cannot be; a responsibility must be limited and must have a level of priority. Without such definitions, the phenomenon of responsibility would simply become a manner of speaking. Consequentialists would say, for example, that my duty to keep a promise I made to someone is not because I have a responsibility to that person, but rather my responsibility is to preserve the good of something (that is, the concept of a promise) from which all people benefit. It follows, then, that a promise should be made to a dying man to comfort him, but whether it is kept or not comes down to purely practical considerations. If nobody benefits from keeping the promise, then the promise alone, as a fact, means nothing at all. From the consequentialist point of view, the act of adultery is quite insignificant. If it brings satisfaction to the parties concerned, and if the other marriage partner consents or has no knowledge of it, then no damage is done; on the contrary, it brings increased worth in the form of greater satisfaction into the world. This view goes against our basic moral instincts. Marriage vows do not mean that you promise not to hurt your partner by revealing your unfaithfulness. Marriage vows mean that you promise to remain faithful. The promise is kept by doing what was promised, not just by pretending to do it. It must be made clear that responsibility for a specific good deed to a specific person can only be accepted when we have no overriding responsibility for the consequences of things we omit to do due to our primary responsibility. A married man is not responsible for a woman committing suicide when he could have prevented it by sleeping with her. One man is not responsible for the death of a hundred men whom he could have freed by murdering one innocent man.

Absolute duties of omission relieve us from responsibility for events we could have changed by intervening when moral or physical reasons prevented us from doing so. An absolute responsibility can exist only when a person is released from all other responsibilities. Responsibility may stand or fall within its parameters, according to what the ancient scholars called the *ordo amoris.* Thomas Aquinas gives us an example of this.[10] A judge, he writes, is bound to pursue the criminal in order to bring him to judgment. The wife of a criminal, on the other hand, is duty-bound to help her husband, if he is trying to hide. The judge's concern is for public safety; the wife's is for her family's well-being. Neither is directly responsible for the universal well-being, which is much more God's concern. Therefore, Thomas tell us, it is not our duty to want what God wants, but rather to want what God wants us to want. We will learn what God's will is by looking back afterward, and both the judge and the woman can be considered good Christians by calmly accepting the failure of their efforts. Martin Luther also writes in this vein: "It is a sure sign of bad will when someone cannot accept not getting his own way."[11]

Grading responsibilities is something we have all come across in professional codes of behavior. A judge responsible for law and order cannot condemn an innocent man for his so-called higher political considerations. A doctor responsible for the health of a patient in his care would breach the medical profession's code of ethics by treating his patient according to whether curing him was desirable for his family and colleagues, or by using his expertise purely to serve the politically defined common good. Similarly, the priest hearing confession may not sacrifice the seal of this confession to some higher responsibility, for example, by exposing a murderer to prevent further crimes.

Consequentialist ethics are free of any deontological restrictions and effectively dispense with the concept of responsibility. This is not only with regard to the object of the action, which, contrary to classical tradition, is also considered to be the purpose of the action, but also in regard to conditions leading up to and surrounding the action. These conditions relating to an action apply to all situations and as such are considered *norms.* There are two types of norms: cultural norms and natural, anthropological norms. Cultural norms are variable and therefore are sometimes hidden by the responsibility of a person's action. No justification is needed to follow a cultural norm unless it directly opposes the basic anthropological norm, that is, is seen as abnormal in this context. In this case, "Man must obey God before men." On the other hand, we are not responsible for natural norms. Therefore, *ab ovo*, there is no burden of proof. This is true with regard to legal authorities, for example. When we are ordered to do something obviously unjust, we must disobey. However, we are not required to test everything beforehand. If we cannot presume that legal authorities act justly, there would be no political order. Action can only be undertaken when there are accepted behavioral norms freeing the agent from having to justify constantly his actions. This is also true of natural norms. When we restrict the liberty of someone carrying an infectious disease, we are not responsible for this discrimination. We are simply drawing the necessary consequences of a given fact. Or, consider the theme of "responsible parenthood." Conceiving a child is not a total, unconditional responsibility but is constrained by things for which we are not responsible; namely, that a child is conceived as the natural consequence of sexual intercourse. There may be reasons for restricting the number of children we have, but if not, then we don't really need any encouragement to procreate. Such a burden of proof would be expecting too much of us. The uncertainty of the future and the child's unknown fate are certainly not sufficient reasons for not bringing a child into the world, just as sufficient grounds never can be given for killing an innocent person. Fortunately, we do not need a reason, or rather, any reason is good enough, providing there is no important reason against. The duty of justification is not symmetrical. Meanwhile, in the West, the contraceptive pill has brought with it a new "norm" that counteracts the natural process and has created the idea of having to "decide" about having children. What's more, widespread use of the pill has meant that men simply shrug off the responsibility for unwanted pregnancies onto women (especially in extramarital relationships), and there is the silent expectation that a woman is on the pill. But only nature has the right to remain silent. Every other norm that assumes the role of nature is tyrannical.

Doing What Is Right in Your Own Affairs

For reasons given at the beginning of the paper, the maxim "Do what is right in your own affairs, and the rest will take care of itself" runs into hefty objections nowadays. It no longer seems clear what exactly *is* "the right thing." In the meanwhile, "the rest" seems to take less and less care of itself, and while everyone is busy fulfilling his limited responsibilities, the overall situation–the basic social and living conditions of people all over the world–becomes continually more precarious. The inevitable outcome of all this would seem to be a globalization of our responsibilities. This in itself does not mean breaking down the structure of our responsibilities and removing the priorities they impose through simple *ordo amoris.* "Let all our actions be for the good of everybody" writes St. Paul, "especially those who belong to the household of the faith" (Galatians 6:10). This rule counts just as much as before. "Let us do good to all people, especially fellow countrymen." This rule is still binding on politicians, who take an oath of office to work for the well-being of their country. They must come to realize that there is a steadily growing interdependence between this well-being and that of other countries. Politicians must see that beneficial progress in their own countries minimizes the harmful consequences to others. But they are not accountable to everyone in the same way. Responsibility for the consequences of cumulative effects–more or less harmless when considered individually–is a problem for them as for any individual. It cannot be solved by loading the responsibility for such cumulative effects onto each individual. Morally, that would be expecting too much. When specific effects–ecological, economic, or social–are identified, someone has to be found, or a body formed, and made responsible for controlling these effects. For example, a body may have global responsibility for a global effect, or at least for making and maintaining a binding international agreement to this effect. Ordinarily, individual states are responsible for regional effects, and they must establish a legal framework for their own private developments. In a democracy all citizens must recognize their moral responsibility. In other words, they cannot bribe the legislator for the sake of their private interests. They must keep the law as they go about their daily business and, in certain circumstances, even contribute to and organize local civic activities for common concerns. In a democracy it is often such civic action that paves the way for state action–as has often been the case with ecological causes, for example.

The private citizen, however, cannot be made morally responsible for the effects of an action that combines and accumulates with those of others on a massive scale. The state cannot be said to have met its responsibility if, for example–with direct reference to the ozone layer–instead of setting up legislation, it just appeals to our individual moral responsibility. Laying all the world's problems directly on the individual conscience in this way will lead to a moral collapse, because the burden is too great for one person to carry. Concrete responsibility then disintegrates into ineffectual moral rhetoric.

When discussing the theme of responsibility, it is impossible to ignore the idea of "doing the right thing in your own affairs." However, from time to time it has to be reviewed because of technical progress–in the field of medical practice, for example. Of course, such a review only makes sense when there are unchanging standards of right and wrong, good and evil, standards by which we can "put our clocks right" now and again. If there were no such thing as the basic structure of human nature, whereby certain things are considered reasonable or unreasonable, then the command to love one another would be meaningless and could be replaced by whatever we wanted. This fundamental nonvariable is what enables us to perceive any sense of responsibility, and we call it the natural moral law. The sense of this theory cannot be explained in more detail at this point and should, so to speak, be expressed merely as a postulate. If I am to accept a responsibility, then there must be criteria by which I can see whether I have acted responsibly or irresponsibly. And I am not responsible for these criteria, because that would mean setting further criteria to decide whether I have determined the criteria in a responsible manner, and so on. Neither does it help to follow one's conscience. A conscientious action means following what is truly held to be an objective standard of right and wrong. Such a belief or conviction is not based on itself but rather on something else. The same is true of our conscience. Conscience is not a given guideline, rule, or measure, but an inner voice that tells us to do what we "recognize" to be right. Conscience is the voice of practical reason. Therefore, a judgment of conscience can only be made by someone who is ready to discuss it with others and to listen to opposing points of view. This discussion, on the other hand, may cause a judgment of conscience to break down if the two parties cannot come to terms. It is always up to the individual to decide when he has examined the matter sufficiently and reached a satisfactory conclusion. Even Christ discussed the theme of good and evil with the devil. But he also ended the discussion with the words "Away with you, Satan."

If conscience were merely considered a subjective authority, not comparable with objective, rational standards, it would be impossible for the state to identify with the national conscience. On the one hand, the state could not allow a citizen to break the law and damage the common good simply because his conscience tells him to do so. Yet the state cannot judge whether this appeal of the conscience is justified or not, because there are no objective guidelines to define a judgment of conscience, or to decide when our conscience is right or wrong. For this reason, although the state cannot always observe conscience, neither can it ignore it for fear of being considered totalitarian. No one can be expected to act against his conscience—conflict would become inevitable, and there would be no hope of a solution.

If we consider conscience as a means of detecting an objective moral order, there may also be conflicts, but theoretically these would be opposing points of view arising from rational discussion. When a legitimate government requires respect for the law, then the laws are fundamentally considered legal and reasonable, and it is wrong to break them. No conscience-discounts are given to terrorist murderers.

Nevertheless, there is one area where most civilized countries legally guarantee tolerance toward conscientious objectors, and that is compulsory military service. Here conscientious objections are recognized as such, although, of course, the state could not accept such reasons coming into general use or military service would have to be abolished. Even the Catholic Church, while recognizing military service, still requires that conscientious objectors be excused. How are we to understand this exception from the general rule?

In my opinion, there is only one answer to this question: a state has an overall duty to defend itself, just as mankind has an overall duty to worship God. But although priests are needed, it does not follow that everyone should be forced to become a priest; by the same token, although soldiers are needed, no one should be forced into it. Of course, every citizen must do his part in defending his country, but killing is not something everyone should be considered capable of. Even in places where the death penalty is considered just and necessary, not every citizen is required to serve as executioner. Compulsory military service is an achievement of democracy, but maybe a bad and totalitarian one. A soldier needs a special ethos and has a special kind of honor. The question remains: Is this damaged when a soldier no longer chooses his profession, like a priest? It seems to me that the right of conscientious objection is nothing more than an expression of doubt as to the validity of compulsory military service. It is worth noting that in *Institutioni Juris Ecclesiasticii* the conservative Cardinal Ottaviani calls compulsory military service a "maxima injuria."

In their so-called "*Königsteiner Erklärung*," the Catholic bishops of Germany described practical dissent from the Catholic teaching on contraception as a matter of personal conscience and, by doing so, threw their own doubt on the truth of this teaching. Otherwise the declaration would be a banality that applied to every moral norm. Why can it not be said that breaking the commandment "Thou shalt not kill" is also a matter of personal conscience? Because we know that murder is a crime and that someone who commits a murder for reasons of conviction will be told by the church that he must change his convictions. When, instead, this person is told to follow his convictions, then it means the church is not convinced of the truth of its own teachings. The same is true when the Catholic Church advises divorced and remarried people to receive Holy Communion as their conscience instructs them. This is another way of saying that the church no longer believes that marriages cannot be dissolved. It would never be written that indiscriminate promiscuity while receiving communion is a matter of personal conscience. It appears that the theme of conscience is carefully introduced when one feels on shaky ground. But that is a misuse of the term. It would be better to say that "in this area, we cannot make a general rule to say what is right and what is wrong. There is a margin for discretion, for weighing the benefits, a choice the individual must make in carrying out certain responsibilities." This is how philosophers would talk. I sometimes think that

Catholic theologians avoid speaking this way because they don't want to contradict the teachings of the church formally, and so they use the word *conscience* as their "black box."

As a rule, the natural moral law does not tell us what we have to do. Human nature is such that we are capable of judging situations and finding our own creative solutions to problems. Neither does the gospel absolve us of this: "Who appointed me a judge or an arbiter between you?" (Luke 12:14) replies Jesus when the disciples ask him to settle a legal dispute. All the same, human nature does show us what we may never do if we are to remain at peace with ourselves and not damage our personal integrity. Consequentialist ethics is peculiar in that it finds no purpose for personal integrity. My responsibility to myself is no greater than my responsibility toward anyone else. Two doctors in the 1950s, charged with actively helping to murder mentally ill patients in Germany during World War II, argued that preventing two crimes by committing one crime is the same as committing no crime. In a clinic for the mentally ill, they drew up lists of patients to be killed. The doctors presented a plausible case that they were actually saving numerous other patients' lives, especially by deporting them to religious hospices. If they had refused to take part in these murderous activities, then, presumably, keener Nazi doctors would have been employed instead. The Supreme Court recognized this as an extenuating circumstance, but the doctors were nevertheless found guilty, as according to Christian-European ethics, no one can be permitted to commit murder, even when it is to prevent something worse from happening.[12] It was not by chance that the court appealed to the Christian understanding of ethics. Christian moral teaching makes me specifically responsible for the person directly affected by my action, and who in this way defines the basic nature of my action. Furthermore, Christian ethics recognizes the responsibility a person has toward himself and his own integrity.

In this respect, the church could find itself faced with a radical decision to make in the near future. More and more people are voicing the opinion that euthanasia should be reintroduced for the severely mentally handicapped and senile. A legal solution has been proposed whereby under certain specific circumstances such killings may become legal. However, this is only on condition that the patient's caretakers (nurses and relatives)—who carry a greater burden than a woman during her nine-month pregnancy, for example–first attend a counseling clinic to discuss the problem. Afterward, should those concerned still wish to proceed with ending the patient's life, a certificate would be issued by the clinic to confirm that counseling has taken place. The doctors then would be free to proceed without risk of prosecution. The question is, would the German Catholic Church let itself be implicated with organized euthanasia in this way, albeit with the good intention of saving lives? If it maintains the Christian convictions held until now by both East and West, then the answer is no. However, it is feared that the church will agree, as it has already decided in favor of this form of cooperation for abortions. It may be that the issue of euthanasia will show those responsible exactly what is at stake, and, when faced with the reality of this "slippery slope," they may reverse their existing decision.

A decision based on integrity, rather than on the principle that the ends justifies the means, obviously depends on belief in God. In an essay entitled "The Grounds for Our Belief in a Divine Ruler of the World,"[13] Fichte shows that, without such belief, moral action would be impossible, because no one could know whether, in the long term, his moral actions had harmful consequences. If we cannot trust that "in all things God works for the good of those who love him" (Romans 8:28), then, in the end, we must take over the role of God and try and ensure the *bonum universi*–even when, as in the case of Marxist-Leninism, many millions of lives were sacrificed in vain, because ultimately it failed. One way or the other, human responsibility can only be sustained along the lines of doing "the right thing in your own affairs," even when "your affair" is not anything fixed and straightforward.

Even complex, overlapping responsibilities remain limited. The ultimate and unconditional responsibility is always to one's own integrity. The martyrs who, along with the apostles, built the foundations of the church, were put to death because they refused to burn a little grain of incense. This refusal had no consequentialist or utilitarian basis. The martyrs were not concerned with the future of the church but with God's commands and their salvation. This attitude has blessed the church with a future that so far has lasted two thousand years. During this time it often has been accused of "salvation egoism." In the 1940s and 1950s a number of novels were published in which men sold their souls. At the time, Karl Rahner wrote an important article condemning this kind of "mysticism of sin."[14] The best text on this theme can be found in Jean-Paul Sartre's posthumous *Cahiers pour une morale*.[15] Sartre writes that for an atheist, thoughts of personal integrity can only be what he admits to himself as pharisaical, moral selfishness. An atheist can only be guided in his actions by their overall consequences. The believer, on the other hand, understands that his responsibility not to damage his own personal integrity is something that has been entrusted to him. For the believer, living a good life is not an act of selfishness but rather shows the glory of God.

It could hardly be said more clearly, and it is rarely stated as such by any moral theologian. The wise virgins from Jesus's parable could also be called selfish because they did not share their oil (Matthew 25:9ff.). But why not? Because they could see that there wouldn't be enough to go round. The lamps would go out before the bridegroom arrived. The virgins' first responsibility was for the light–their own light. The command to "keep oneself uncontaminated by the world" (James 1:27) is not from some bigoted nineteenth-century author, but from the New Testament. And at Pentecost, when the people ask Peter, "What must we do?," he replied "Save yourselves from this corrupt generation" (Acts 2:40). In this respect our responsibility is for charity to begin at home. According to St. Thomas, the love of God does not cancel out the *ordo amoris*, which gives priorities to our responsibilities, but rather restores it.[16] The fact that modern ethics barely recognizes a person's duty to himself is reflected by the latent atheism of our times. When I am only answerable to myself for everything I do, and I consider my responsibility to myself above all else, then it makes no sense to say that I am responsible *for* myself. Maybe I have a duty to look after myself because I am important to another person. But, as a rule, that concerns my physical rather than my moral integrity. And what if there is no other person to whom I am important? Unconditional responsibility to oneself must be absolute and unquestioned in all circumstances and therefore independent of me. A person's responsibility to himself, for what used to be called "saving his soul," restricts his options. All the physical possibilities for solving a problem are no longer open; some are impossible for moral reasons. A free man can be recognized, because he does not "have his price" for everything.

Neither tyrants nor any reasons of state can prevent Antigone from fulfilling her duty to bury her brother, and she is ready to die for this cause. This deontological fundamentalism makes her the forerunner of those free people who choose to resist totalitarianism.

Overstretching the ethics of responsibility has led to simple ethics of conviction being considered irresponsible. We have a responsibility to ourselves and, among other things, this comes from our natural human make-up. It is this responsibility that sets the limit for every other responsibility. This moral boundary becomes a physical boundary, then overstepping it becomes not only a "may not" but a "cannot"–and for the better. For then we must speak of character–and this limits our flexibility. Only those who are prepared to do a great deal, but yet not everything, deserve to have responsibility entrusted to them.

Notes

1. Max Weber, *Politik als Beruf* (Berlin, 1919). English translation in *From Max Weber: Essays in Sociology*, ed. H. H. Gerth and C. Wright Mills (New York, 1946).

2. See H. Jonas, *Das Prinzip Verantwortung* (Frankfurt a.M., 1979). English edition: *The Imperative of Responsibility: In Search of an Ethics for the Technological Age* (Chicago and London, 1984).

3. See F. X. Kaufmann, "Über die soziale Funktion von Verantwortung and Verantwortlichkeit," in *Verantwortlichkeit und Recht (Jahrbuch für Rechtssozialogie und Rechtstheorie*, vol. 14), ed. E. J. Lampe (Opladen, 1989), pp. 204-224.

4. J. W. Goethe, *Spruche*, vol. 1 (Hamburger Ausgabe), p. 314.

5. See Thomas Aquinas, *Quaestio Disputata de Malo 6*; see R. Spaemann, "Nebenwirkungen als moralisches Problem," in *Zur Kritik der politischen Utopie* (Stuttgart, 1977), p. 172.

6. I. Kant, *Grundlegung zur Metaphysik der Sitten*, A 23 *(Akad.-Ausg.*, BDIV), p. 405.

7. See R. Spaemann, "Über die Unmöglichkeit einer universalteleologischen Ethik," in *Philosophisches Jahrbuch* 88 (1981), pp. 70-89; idem, "Wer hat wofür Verantwortung?," in *Herder Korrespondenz* 36 (July-August 1982).

8. See R. Spaemann, "Über die Unmöglichkeit einer universalteleologischen Ethik."

9. *De Divinis Nominibus IV*, 30; *Patrologia Graeca* 3, 729.

10. Thomas Aquinas, *Summa Theologiae* I-III q. 19, art. 10.

11. Martin Luther, *Ausgewählte Werke*, vol. 1, ed. Borcherdt and Merz (Munich, 1951), p. 319.

12. German Supreme Court, Judgment of 28 November 1952.

13. GA I 5, pp. 347-357.

14. Karl Rahner, "Situationsethik und Sündenmystik," in *Stimmen der Zeit* 145 (1947/50), pp. 330-342.

15. J. Sartre, *Cahiers pour une morale* (Paris, 1983), p. 11.

16. Thomas Aquinas, *Summa Theologiae* II q. 26, a.13.

7

Pastoral Practice and Conscience

Ignacio Carrasco de Paula

The encyclical *Veritatis Splendor* begins the section on moral conscience with the observation that the contrast between law and freedom as it is formulated by some contemporary thinkers leads to "a 'creative' understanding of moral conscience, which diverges from the teaching of the church's tradition and her Magisterium."[1] Slightly further on it adds that on the basis of this idea, which is foreign to Christian morality, "an attempt is made to legitimize so-called 'pastoral' solutions contrary to the teaching of the Magisterium, and to justify a 'creative' hermeneutic according to which the moral conscience is in no way obliged, in every case, by a particular negative precept."[2]

I consider it opportune to begin with this reference to the document of John Paul II, simply because I have not found a better way of defining the subject matter assigned to me. It is, indeed, not my intention to discuss the problem of the creativity of conscience in depth; other colleagues have done that with the highest skill. Rather, my intention is to analyze and come to a discernment about certain proposals stemming from pastoral concern, which have tried to harmonize the faith and morality of the church with the difficulties encountered by the faithful, difficulties that at times are great and even dramatic. However, these proposals either presuppose or end up in an erroneous interpretation of the function of conscience.

As a first step it is necessary to make clear what we should understand by the term *pastoral solution*. But first, I wish to establish a premise. The pastoral sphere is not an area proper to philosophers and theologians to debate about, as colleagues, knowing that what is at stake is simply trying to get closer to the truth. The pastoral sphere is within the competence of pastors; that is to say, those people whom Christ has sacramentally associated with his mission as the Good Shepherd. They are authoritatively constituted ministers within the church; their role is to govern a part of the People of God. They enjoy a dignity, which, precisely because it does not rest on personal merit but on the *munus* they fulfill, makes them worthy of the highest respect and veneration.

In short, I wish to make it clear that the object of this essay is neither the systematic study of the pastoral action of the church (which is inseparable from her saving mission) nor an analysis of certain provisions made in fact, decisions taken by legitimate pastors acting within their proper jurisdiction. Therefore the evocation of real or imaginary episodes of recent ecclesiastical history remains foreign to my intentions.

What Is Meant by "Pastoral Solution"?

Within the church we usually use *pastoral action* to refer to that service which sacred ministers perform, a service guided by the principle of the *salus animarum* or, if you prefer, the implanting of the Reign of God in souls. Pastors must lead the faithful to full participation in the life that God has wished to communicate through his Son. They must promote and facilitate the access to redemption, which Christ has achieved through his life, death, and resurrection.

Each pastoral activity always implies a praxis, an operative strategy of greatest efficacy in the proclamation of the word, administration of the sacraments, liturgical prayer, regulation of the morals and behavior of the faithful, et cetera. Pastoral criteria should not be confused with simple pragmatic guidelines or working hypotheses, or still less with the experience and contribution of the behavioral sciences such as sociology, psychology, and so on. All of these constitute sources, more or less valid, that should be weighed with greatest attention and adaptability. The *salus animarum*, however, is totally bound to the gospel and to ecclesial realities, on which it depends entirely. The salvation of man is not a sort of "great city" to which all the roads of the earth seem indiscriminately to lead. Christ uses the metaphor of the fishing net (Matthew 13:47-50), which gathers every type of fish, but he reminds us that once the shore is reached, the good are separated from the bad.

Salvation is achieved only through faith and personal adherence to the incarnate Word, realized and perfected in the church he founded. "Under heaven there is no other name"–Peter declares before the Sanhedrin–"given to men by which they can be saved" (Acts 4:12). The church has expressed this conviction in the ancient phrase *extra ecclesiam nulla salus*, in which she declares her vocation of being the efficacious sign of liberation for all of humanity. This vocation is neither exclusivist nor elitist (although this erroneous interpretation has caused the phrase to fall into disuse).

For each and every living person salvation is the decisive event. "Of what use is it to a man if he has gained the whole world but loses or ruins himself?" (Luke 9:25). For this reason in the discernment of the *signa temporum,* the pastoral point of view retains an indisputable primacy, which the church has known how to administer with prudence.

The church has always been aware of two facts: on the one hand, she has the duty to proclaim unceasingly "Christ crucified, scandal for the Jews, folly for the Gentiles" (1 Corinthians 1:23). On the other hand, she knows that the Holy Spirit, by whom she is governed, *ubi vult spirat* (John 3:8). The Spirit breathes where it wills, not infrequently making nonsense of human prognostications and predictions. The church is not a "factory" of saints but rather the tangible presence of divine love among men.

The church lives a perennial paradox. She has the disposition of a mother and knows when to be indulgent. On occasion, however, she historically has had to pronounce with firmness a *non possumus,* even foreseeing not only the tragedy of the blood of innocent martyrs but, above all, the anguishing menace of lacerations that would distance entire peoples from the sources of grace. On other occasions she has had to react so that no hireling would obstruct the gateway or would make even narrower the path that leads to life (cf. Matthew 7:14) by overtaxing the consciences of the faithful with imaginary burdens that would be contrary to the liberty with which Christ has set us free (cf. Galatians 5:1). The church has always kept in mind the example of her Master who, using a metaphor that the rabbis of his time used in reference to the obligations of the Mosaic law, defined the moral commitment imposed on his disciples as an easy yoke and a light burden (cf. Matthew 11:28).

The pastoral solutions to which the encyclical refers generally stem from the attempt to resolve certain conflicts of conscience by freeing the faithful from obligations that are held to be not absolutely certain and indispensable or, at least, by attempting to lessen the burden through an attitude of tolerance *hic et nunc* that has the aim of seeking full compliance in the future. In order to illustrate this better, I would like to cite the words of Tullo Goffi, an Italian moralist most noted for his pastoral concern: "It would be neither human nor Christian to expect that the (onanist) spouse necessarily be capable of living totally in the spirit, as if he were already totally risen in Christ."[3]

A Legal and Theological Problem

This type of practical remedy sets up a double problem: legal and theological. On the one hand, the duty of serving souls with a view to their salvation has to be carried out within the limits of the power that God has given to his church, a power that covers the area from the custody, interpretation, and transmission of the deposit of revelation (faith and morals) to the power of the keys. Christ has given to his pastors the power to absolve sins, but not the power to establish arbitrarily where vice and virtue lie. Furthermore, pardon is not the magic result of the mechanical dispensation of a rite; it always demands the free and considered consent of the penitent in the act of repentance.

On the other hand, the ministry to souls should be in conformity with the theological reality it seeks to realize. This principle leads moral theologian Bernard Häring to point out, in carefully chosen words, "that it is illegitimate and probably a great injustice to impose very heavy burdens on people in the name of God, unless it is completely clear that this is the will of God." This most just affirmation should be read in the light of another much less attractive principle: it is equally damaging to render vain the salvific will of God by authorizing types of behavior that in and of themselves exclude one from eternal salvation.

The legal and moral aspects have their own proper areas of competence and autonomy, but they are not totally independent spheres. Each offers to the other a complementary view of the same reality. The distinction between the two is not always easy to determine, especially in regard to the prescriptions developed by the church with a finality that is specifically pastoral. Until recent decades, positive ecclesiastical law enjoyed a privileged attention from moral science. Today, on the other hand, it has almost disappeared from view. We are very happy to turn over this area to our canonical colleagues. Independently of our own tastes and preferences, however, ecclesiastical law obliges in conscience, with a greater or lesser force according to the nature of the precept—its connection with divine law—and the will of the lawmaker. Conflicts may also arise here, especially when it is a question of definitions that are changeable, contingent, or dependent on the circumstances of time, culture, and so on. This is the case, for example, with some instructions regarding discipline, liturgy, and more.

In any event, returning to the double theological-legal difficulty, I think that the problems of conscience that some "pastoral solutions" have tried to eliminate in an erroneous manner can be classified into two types:

1. a conflict between a moral norm—for example, that contraception is "intrinsically wrong" (*Humanae Vitae*, no. 14)—and the belief that it is impossible to observe it, which would take away all obligation (*ad impossibilia nemo tenetur*);

2. a conflict between an ecclesiastical prohibition—for example that of "not admitting to eucharistic communion divorced people who have remarried" (*Familiaris Consortio*, no. 84)—and the conviction of a person who believes he is unjustly discriminated against because, for example, he is convinced that his first marriage was not in fact valid, even though it is not possible to prove this before the competent tribunal.

Moral Systems: A Precedent?

If by pastoral solutions we are referring to a method of resolving morally uncertain cases, we would have to acknowledge that there already exists a venerable tradition of the church in this regard. The nearest point of reference is in the moral systems developed at the end of the sixteenth century. As is well known, these give a collection of complex deductions and hypotheses that sought to offer a ready solution for the Christian who, though determined not to sin, is undecided between obligation and freedom: the *pars tutior* (in favor of the law) and the *pars favens libertati* (in favor of liberty).

The moral dilemma was held to be unsolvable from the theoretical point of view. This means that the *auctores probati* excluded the questions explicitly decided by arguments from revelation or from the Magisterium. But where certainty was lacking, they sought a way out. It consisted in identifying a pragmatic criterion that, although not directly and in itself revealing the true moral value at issue, at least permitted the subject to act without fear of falling formally into sin. In this way a sophisticated ponderation of opinions was listed, ordered according to a scale of greater or lesser probability. It is not clear whether the *auctores probati* sought to formulate a certain judgment or simply to facilitate decision, especially in cases of perplexed, hesitating, and unresolved conscience.

A fixed element in these solutions was the so-called *principia reflexa.* I shall cite some of those more frequently used: *in dubio favendum est reo; in dubio favores sunt ampliandi et odia restringenda; in dubiis, quod minimum est tenendum* . . . . They are rules borrowed from the treasury of the jurist. Certainly they make sense in the penal area, but only with great caution can they be applied to true conflicts of conscience. In the first place, this is because they presuppose a dialectic between law and liberty that is foreign to Christian ethics. Second, because they take it for granted that the relationship between moral truth and the judgment of conscience is highly problematic and uncertain.

Perhaps it might be pertinent to recall an example from St. Thomas. In the *quodlibeta* he confronts a question that was much discussed in his time: whether it is a mortal sin to accumulate, without the relevant dispensation, various benefices not burdened with the care of souls.[4] This is a typical example of an uncertain law. Nevertheless, Thomas does not free himself by means of the easy path, taking shelter behind a principle, but he examines the positions—*oportet esse alteram veram et alteram falsam*—in order to conclude in accordance with the moral values that are in play.

Behind the questions that we are treating, there stands a mental *habitus* that evaluates the moral law and penal measures with the same ruler.

The Disputed Model

The pastoral solutions that *Veritatis Splendor* points out to be contrary to the Christian tradition do not have much to do with what have been called, perhaps too pompously, moral systems, and now are viewed in much more moderate terms. Their proposals are characterized by the following elements:

1. First of all, a moral or disciplinary norm is recognized–usually a specific negative precept–authentically declared or confirmed by the Magisterium, which proposes it as obligatory in conscience for all the church's faithful.

2. On the other hand, a discrepancy can be detected between the goods indicated and protected by the norm and the actual behavior of the faithful.

3. This divergence is interpreted as revealing not only human weakness, which cannot always avoid sin, but also an internal rupture between the comprehension of the declaration of a law and the perception of one's own individual circumstances. The faithful affected by this problem will feel crushed by a conflict of duties or by the impossibility of literally obeying the precept.

4. This internal conflict–which vaguely recalls the Freudian concept of ambivalence–would cause an unbearable tension, even for believers of good will. Little by little it would undermine their confidence in the pastors and lead them to abandon religious practice, later to resentment, then to indifference, and finally, to apostasy. In short, it would lead to self-exclusion from the plan of salvation. In support of these somber predictions, worrying statistical data are sometimes quoted, as, for example, the number of people who abandon the church each year. Normally, however, a comparative analysis of the deleterious effects freedom of conscience has in the pagan world is omitted.

5. Posing the problem in this way, it is suggested that a pragmatic criterion be found that will allow people in crisis to remain in the

church and to exercise fully their rights as *christifideles*, which in concrete terms means admission to the sacraments.

In theory, one remedy could be to restrict the universal and absolute value of the contested norms by allowing some exceptions. This is a line that has been followed by some theologians. But this has not seemed very convincing for pastoral workers, because it does not solve the problem but merely moves a little further the limits beyond which conscience may not go.

The definitive and final resolution is proposed as follows: 1) Given that the judgment of conscience is the proximate norm of the morality of a voluntary act, 2) given that this judgment has an imperative and unquestionable character (one has to act in accordance with it, even if it is corrupted by invincible error), 3) and given that it represents the inviolable intimacy of the person, 4) it must be deduced that each person should be allowed to follow the dictates of his own conscience, even when it contradicts a precept established by the church and the person is conscious of this.

Here is an example of reasoning along these lines:

> It seems absurd that the church requires parents to be responsible and, at the same time, tells them that there is no method that makes this responsibility possible. . . . If parents have a child, even when it was not prudent for them to have one, they do not sin. And, if they use a method that in itself is not appropriate, while they wait for the scientists to discover another that is, they do not sin. It is something the husband and wife must decide according to their own consciences without any kind of pressure. And, whatever decision is taken, they must in no way be deprived of the sacraments. Neither should they even confess, because, in reality, they have not sinned.[5]

On reaching this point, it appears necessary to make some clarifications:

1. It is clear that this position goes further than a simple application of traditional doctrine on the invincibly erroneous conscience. No one questions the possibility that one or many specific people may resort to a contraceptive procedure without knowing that it is immoral and, therefore, without sin being imputed to them. The problem is whether it is licit to present an explicit moral norm, definitely

established by the Magisterium, and then conclude that those who think that it is not reasonable to accept it are dispensed from it.

2. It is not a question, either, of extending the privileges granted in the sacrament of penance to people who are completely ignorant of the moral issue. Faced with a spiritually illiterate person (while making a case-by-case judgment), the confessor may remain silent, for the time being, about the true evil of an act, if he judges that by acting differently the only result would be that what is now a material sin would become a formal sin. It is a very different thing, however, to approve an erroneous judgment, attributing to individual conscience a power that it does not truly possess, while thinking that in this way the responsibility of the disobedient faithful would be taken away.

Deciding in Conscience

It is possible that what I have said up to now will not provoke too much reaction in those who think that it is licit to decide deliberately against the letter of the law according to one's conscience. That, however, which they certainly will not be disposed to admit is that their version of the privileges of conscience, *man's sanctuary*,[6] is incompatible with Christian morality. In this regard they advance several claims in their defense (which I have summarized in three propositions) that merit examination.

The first thesis recognizes that conscience is not above the moral law and does not constitute a parallel and independent judgment. Nevertheless, it is the ultimate court that interprets the concrete meaning of the general rule–divine or ecclesiastical–and decides its practical application. Moreover, it does so in a variety of situations that a higher legislator would have difficulty in taking into account.

According to this thesis it would seem that conscience could not err, or at least that it would be impossible to know if it has erred. In cases in which the judgment of conscience seems to be putting itself in contradiction to the law, in reality it would be rendering explicit an implicit duty.

The second thesis confirms that conscience must not act arbitrarily. It must reason in a responsible context, analogously, for example, to the model that *Gaudium et Spes* proposed with regard to the demographic problem in its time. Thus,[7] presupposing an attitude of obedient reverence to God, the correct judgment of conscience is formed by reflecting on 1) our own good and that of others who morally depend on us; 2) the circumstances of the historical moment and our own condition, both material and spiritual; and 3) the safeguarding of the just hierarchy of the goods in the family, society, and church.

With regard to the interpretation and the use made of the conciliar text, the least that can be said is that they are singular. Clearly they are partial. Some authors do not seem to be aware of the fact that, in defining responsible parenthood, the Council (for the reasons indicated in the note added to no. 51 by order of Paul VI) limited itself to identifying some external points of reference but did not wish to enter into the merits of the question. Furthermore, the Council did not neglect to affirm that "the conscience ought to be conformed to the law of God in the light of the teaching authority of the church, which is the authentic interpreter of the divine law,"[8] and also that it is necessary to "avoid all solutions which transgress the moral law."[9]

The third thesis recognizes that conscience may err, and even denounces the fact that in modern society there are trends that repress the autonomy of judgment of the faithful. Nevertheless, they do not seek to justify the error but only to overcome the doubt (to my way of thinking, this distinction is essential in order not to interpret the "pastoral" solutions superficially). Therefore, pastoral action should not only support responsible decisions taken by the faithful who are in delicate and difficult situations but should contribute to overcoming uncertainty by discerning the *true* will of God, which is present in the law.

One way to do this could be, for example, along the lines of what *The Catechism of the Catholic Church* (no. 1788) says about the advice of experienced persons who help to interpret the data of experience and the signs of the times. But what is the real role of that help? Only to favor reflection, foment critical examination, refine reasoning, question oneself, and so on. That is to say, it consists in acting like a psychotherapist, without interfering, because–again *Gaudium et Spes* is quoted–the final decision corresponds exclusively to the conscience of the interested party.

The following statement by Enrico Chiavacci on the encyclical *Humanae Vitae* can serve as an example:

When the spouses possess sufficient spiritual formation and Christian culture, in such a way that they can form a well-founded view on the issue in question; when, moreover, they have studied the encyclical with filial love and have honestly tried to convince themselves of its teachings; when any presumption, scandal or publicity is excluded; if in such a hypothesis the spouses reach the conclusion that the norm is theoretically unacceptable, then—and only then—may they behave in practice in accordance with their own conscience and answer before God for the choice they have made.[10]

The Moral Significance of Pastoral Solutions

Although running the risk of appearing excessively schematic, I wish to indicate what, in my opinion, constitute the three critical points of a pastoral strategy that assumes the responsibility of leaving the conscience of the faithful prey to error:

1. *Gnoseological postulate:* Moral law, as understood by Christians, would be substantially unknowable and uncertain. Its formulations in human language could not be more than suggestions. The conscience would run the risk of erring with regard to the law—to the effect of not coinciding with its literal wording—but not with regard to its moral value or, if you prefer, its spirit. When conscience appears to err, in reality it is making up for the gnoseological limits of the norm.

This explains, for example, the fact that he who defends the creativity of conscience stresses the nondefinitive or noninfallible nature of the moral documents of the Magisterium. In reality, what is questioned is not the theological note of an authentic text but the immutability of the moral law itself, as we know it through reason and faith.

2. *Axiological postulate:* Divine and human moral law would be an essentially limiting and burdensome reality. The Magisterium of the church is seen to be increasing the dosage, adopting excessively categorical positions that achieve nothing but the creation of painful and useless psychological and moral conflicts. Consequently, when the various problematic cases are examined in this perspective, the norm almost automatically is placed under accusation, while all kinds of excuses for personal conscience are alleged.

At the root of this mentality there is an underlying ethical voluntarism, which is perfectly in line with the gnoseological postulate. A norm that is epistemologically ungraspable cannot have been generated by divine wisdom but only by a legislative will. Now, there is nothing more irritating than that something which affects me intimately, and almost decides my life, is good or bad because a superior power has so decided. In the name of the freedom that has been granted to me, and that it would be unjust to withdraw from me, I may feel myself authorized to demand to participate in the decisions that affect me. In the game of life I do not dispute the final reward, but at least I should be able to agree to the rules of the game, both to assert my freedom and because the game has infinite combinations, which no regulations can pretend to resolve a priori.

3. *Soteriological postulate:* The Christian moral law–that is to say, the gospel–would not have any connection with salvation except in a generic, almost irrelevant way. This is because pastorally–in the order of the salvation of souls–it makes no difference whether or not conscience conforms to the moral norm, as long as one is not lacking in a will, which is not further defined than as "good." If, in that conformity, no other advantage is seen besides giving witness to an ideal, or of adopting an exemplary or more perfect lifestyle, or of anticipating what will be common eschatalogically to all believers, then one is presupposing that the gospel is irrelevant and the cross of Christ is a decorative motif or at most a premonitory sign (certainly quite a strange one) of the new heavens and the new earth that one day will come to pass, although we do not know how. Salvation, therefore, would be neither a gratuitous fact nor a reward that is in some way due, because it could not be denied to anyone–only human freedom would have the power to reject it–or granted as the crown of a life that has tried to identify itself with the life of Christ.

This point is essential and would merit a more detailed treatment because it shows the Achilles's heel of some "pastoral" hypotheses that, in the name of the *salus animarum,* empty salvation itself of meaning. It would turn out to be only an obscure hope, which the incarnation of the Word had vainly tried to illuminate. It would depend only on an indefinable good will, compatible with concentration camps, ethnic purification, the slaughter of innocents, betrayal, and the refusal to maintain one's promises.

By Way of Conclusion

I have left for the end a question that should perhaps have been asked at the start: Are these extreme cases, the solution of which is desired to be left to the judgment of the interested party, truly conflicts of conscience?

Of course, as we have seen, the starting point is the comparison between the statement of the moral law and the opposing dictate of conscience. It is implicitly taken for granted that this is not just a question of application (if this were so, it would be difficult to talk of opposition), but that it touches on the question of decision, and that this decision arises in a strictly private sphere where no outside influence of any kind is permitted. As a result, it seems that everything is reduced to a conflict of powers, in which the private should prevail over the public, the personal over the impersonal, the practical over the theoretical, the concrete over the abstract. The pastoral solutions are placed in this line of argumentation, when *de facto* they are claiming full moral autonomy for conscience. They superimpose on the relations between God and man a perception of divine freedom as a limit and border of human freedom. A false problem cannot pretend to find an authentic solution, even when the salvation of all men is desired with all the good will in the world, as we who are Christians logically desire.

What then is the question? In the same way that a conflict between a doctor who prescribes insulin for a diabetic when the patient would prefer to take vitamin C is not due to a challenge between two spheres of influence but, rather, between two ways of reasoning (of which one should prevail over the other if the patient wishes to get well), so it is between the law of God and the practical judgment of conscience. In other words, the problem lies in whether or not the "dependence of human reason on divine Wisdom"[11] is recognized, as *Veritatis Splendor* affirms.

No one can deny that one or many moral prescriptions could be considered obscure, unreasonable, difficult, arbitrary, unjust, and so forth, and that this view of things could be more or less shared by a large number of people. It hardly seems worth taking the time to pause at this moment to justify a phenomenon that contradicts only the naive idea that truth, by the very fact of being such, should prevail by itself. Truth does not cease to be such simply because it is widely contested. We need to take a pastoral approach, but it should be a pastoral approach that is done starting from the truth and in the truth of salvation.

The human mind is extraordinarily complicated and is conditioned by innumerable factors, many of which are unknown, and by obscure and distant origins, which go back to original sin. In any case, a service to souls that did not attempt to attract them to the light of Christ, but which left them buried in darkness and confirmed, as it were, in their error, would be a contradiction. The education of conscience, which we all acknowledge to be one of the primary tasks of the pastoral area, demands as a *sine qua non* condition the submission of the created mind to uncreated Wisdom. The word *submission* may not be found pleasing. We may speak, therefore, of adhesion, interiorization, assumption, and so on. But the substance of the task does not change. Error cannot save. Only "the truth will make you free" (John 8:32).

Notes

1. *Veritatis Splendor*, no. 54.
2. *Veritatis Splendor*, no. 56.
3. Tullo Goffi, "Humanae Vitae," *Note Teologico-Pastorali* (Brescia: Queriniana, 1968), p. 97.
4. *Quodlib.* 8, q. 6, a. 3; q. 7, a. 2.
5. Antonio Hortelano, *Amore e Matrimonio: Nuove Prospettive* (Assisi: Cittadella Editrice, n.d.), p. 215.
6. *Gaudium et Spes*, no. 16.
7. See *Gaudium et Spes*, no. 50.
8. *Gaudium et Spes*, no. 50.
9. *Gaudium et Spes*, no. 87.
10. Enrico Chiavacci, *Studi di Teologia Morale* (Assisi: Cittadella Editrice, 1971), p. 203.
11. *Veritatis Splendor*, no. 36.

8

The Autonomy of Conscience and Subjection to Truth

Carlo Caffarra

Introduction

The "fate" that has befallen conscience in Christian ethical thought has been a singular one, as it has moved from what I would not hesitate to call a secondary position to an increasingly central one. It would not be difficult to provide an analytical demonstration of this historical fact; indeed, some research has already been carried out in this respect. However, I do not propose to provide such a demonstration, as this would require historical expertise that I do not possess.[1] I will therefore restrict myself to stating three facts: two that are difficult to contest and a third that is less obvious.

The first fact. In his *Summa Theologica*, St. Thomas Aquinas dedicates only three articles to the theme of conscience: one in the *prima pars* (q.79, a.13) and two in the *prima secundae* (q.19, a.5 and 6). If we now take St. Alfonso's *Theologia Moralis*, we will observe that its general makeup comprises just two sections (*tractatus*), the first dedicated to conscience and the second to law.

In his introduction the Church Doctor writes that by reflecting on conscience "*aditus ad universam theologiam moralem aperitur.*"[2] This affirmation is theoretically sound: the doctrine on conscience enables us to enter into moral reflection. In other words, the doctrine of conscience is the keystone of the entire arch.

There is no doubt whatsoever that we are faced with a real theoretical change, a theoretical transformation within Catholic thought. The question arises as to whether it is what we might call an organic development, which respects the symphonic harmony of the whole, or a pathological development. We will leave this question unanswered for the moment.

The second fact is even more important and more difficult to interpret. We could summarize it as the uprooting of conscience from within the church.

When I read the Church Fathers and the great masters of Christian thought, one of the things that strikes me most profoundly is their awareness of a certain identity between the "individual" and the church. I will illustrate this using just two examples.

In his *Homily on the Canticle of Canticles* (1.7)[3] Origen can say, "I, the church" and the whole of that page is based on this mysterious identification between the thinking subject, that is, the person of the believer, and the church. The church is in the believer and the believer is in the church. In his *Comment on the Canticle of Canticles*,[4] he is therefore able to write: "The bride, that is, the church or the soul that strives toward perfection." You will note that he says "the church or the soul." It has been observed again and again that this mystical identification constitutes the fundamental hermeneutical principle of the Holy Scriptures, which all speak of Christ, that is, the church, that is, every believer.[5]

We also find this in the Middle Ages. One example will suffice here. The whole of St. Bernard's *Commentary on the Canticle of Canticles* is based on this mystical identification. "*Quae est sponsa,*" he asks, "*et quis est sponsus?*" And he answers: "*Hic Deus noster est, et illa, si audeo dicere, nos sumus.*"[6] However, the page in which this experience is perhaps expressed most sublimely is in *Sermon XII,* 11: "*Quod etsi nemo nostrum sibi arrogare praesumat, ut animam suam quis audeat sponsam Domini appellare, quoniam tamen de Ecclesia sumus, quae merito hoc nomine et re nominis gloriatur, non immerito gloriae huius participium usurpamus. Quod enim simul omnes plene integreque possidemus, hoc singuli sine contradictione participamus.*" And he ends with this marvelous prayer:

"*Gratias tibi, Domine Jesu, qui nos carissimae Ecclesiae tuae aggregare dignatus es, non solum ut fideles essemus, sed ut etiam tibi vice sponsae in amplexos iucundos, castos, aeternosque copularemur.*"[7]

As we pursue our line of thinking, St. Bernard's page proves most helpful. He says: "*Quod simul omnes plene integreque possidemus, hoc singuli sine contradictione participamus.*" Our identification with the church is therefore explained in terms of plenitude and wholeness–in other words, it is "catholic." The individual shares in this plenitude and wholeness. He is all the church, even if not totally so. The church becomes the abode or, in other words, the *ethos* of the believer.

This marvelous meeting of the individual and the church begins to be a problem when the church begins to be seen as a reality that is extrinsic to the individual. The ecclesiastical body is no longer a constituent dimension of the individual but a manifestation of God's will that has no foundation in man's individual existence. This results in an ontological separation and an attempt to overcome it through an effort of will (obedience to the church).

We must now look carefully at another text, signed by three German bishops (Saier, Lehmann, and Kasper), concerning the pastoral letter on divorced people who remarry.[8] I refer in particular to the paragraph in which they affirm that under certain conditions a Catholic can legitimately be allowed to receive Holy Communion, even if there is no reason to think that the first consummated marriage was invalid and even if he enjoys sexual union with the person he now lives with. The decision is to be arrived at on the basis of the judgment of conscience. This is an exceptionally serious state of affairs. For the first time in the church's history, the church itself has recognized, through its ministers, that there is no objective sacramental structure that should not be submitted to the final judgment of individual conscience, that there is no structure which should not be verified or cannot be falsified by the judgment of individual conscience. The church must now recognize this verification and falsification as legitimate. Most important of all, the church has always taught that the indissolubility of ratified and consummated marriage (*ratum et consumatum*) is based on divine revelation. The problem is that the three bishops' document, despite explicit affirmations made in the document itself and certainly despite their intentions, may introduce into the Christian community the notion that this divinely revealed teaching can be called into question on the basis of a judgment of conscience. In other words, the truth of a proposition taught by the church as based on revelation must ultimately be submitted to the judgment of conscience.

If we now compare the starting point with the point of arrival, we will see exactly what we mean when we talk about the uprooting of conscience from the church. The separation of church and conscience (that of its own subjectivity) has now gone as far as it can. Is there any relationship between the two facts I have stated so far? In other words, has conscience increasingly assumed the role of "keystone" in the moral edifice precisely because it has increasingly been uprooted from the church? Put yet another way, are we now confronted with a further confirmation of the increasingly radical subjectivism that has characterized the historical event we know as modernity? I will leave this question unanswered for the moment, as I would now like to draw your attention to the third fact, which we have witnessed first-hand, and by so doing draw this long introduction to a close.

The third fact consists of the process known usually as postmodernity, during which the constructed "subject" has gradually been deconstructed. It is not necessary to describe, even briefly, the process by which "subjectivity" has been totally demolished.[9]

I will just briefly outline the way in which this relates to moral conscience. Here, I will have to oversimplify somewhat. I have followed the debate on bioethics fairly closely over the last few years, mostly as a test of more profound changes.[10] The first fact I have observed is that rationality based on utilitarianism and proportionality has now won pride of place in institutional circles (for instance, in the area of civil law), scientific research, and individual spirituality. We know that the choice of this model of rationality means the complete destruction of ethics (as was rightly foreseen by Kant and even more profoundly by Manzoni).[11] As the "weighing-up of each good" in this context is a technical type of judgment, individual conscience has no choice but to place its trust in the judgment of so-called experts. What I mean is this: eventually, conscience finds itself being gradually dispossessed of its hard-won autonomy.

I have said that I have used the debate on bioethics as a test of something more profound. Probably the most profound event is precisely this gradual emptying of conscience. It was Newman who foresaw that we would gradually destroy conscience in the name of conscience. One of the parables of the gospel may provide us with an illustration of this phenomenon, too—in the story of the son who leaves the father to assert himself and ends up working as a swineherd. Is it possible to find a single interpretative key to this tragedy in two acts? He abandons his home (the church) in order to affirm his own autonomy (Act I) and ends up all alone in the countryside looking after pigs (Act II). Is it possible to rediscover the path that will lead Christian subjectivity and conscience back home, so that they are once more one and the same thing? The following two sections will seek to answer both these questions.

Diagnostic Reflection

The whole doctrine of conscience depends on the way in which we answer one central question. Which question? A human being is under no moral obligation unless he knows himself to be so. It is this act of reasoning that "binds" his freedom, and this act is irreplaceable. No authority, whether human or divine, can constrain his freedom except by or through this act of judgment. If autonomy means the inescapable necessity of this mediation, then to deny it is to deny the existence of any moral obligation, indeed that of any morals at all. But the problem lies precisely in this inescapable mediation.

The sentence, "a human being is under no moral obligation unless he knows himself to be so" would seem to imply two different things: the state of being under an obligation and the knowledge that one is under an obligation. The central question to which I referred earlier is precisely this: What is the relationship between the fact of being under an obligation and the fact of knowing oneself to be under an obligation? The whole doctrine of conscience depends on the answer we give to this question.

The solution that modernity has gradually constructed has been simply to identify the two above-mentioned facts—a perfect identification achieved once and for all in transcendental idealism. The exact nature of this identity is the following: placing oneself under an obligation and recognizing that one is under an obligation are one and the same thing.

This identity has both a negative and a positive side: negative, in that the moral obligation never precedes the awareness we have of it in any way; positive, in that it is the act of realizing that one is under an obligation that brings into existence a moral obligation. It is not only the *principium quo* (*fons cognoscendi*), but also the *principium quod* (*fons essendi*) of moral obligation.

However, I do not propose to pursue this theoretical phenomenon into the realm of nontheological thought but into that of Catholic theology. It is obvious that this sort of identification could not pass just as it was into Christian theology, since the logically necessary outcome of this very identification is atheism and sheer amorality—as history has proven. In other words, modernity's answer to this central question on the matter of conscience was in clear contradiction with faith. So what happened? The story is a complex one and its reconstruction and interpretation far from easy.

In the first place, as a great deal of historical research has shown,[12] legalism had profoundly pervaded Catholic ethical thought. There is no need to stop and give a rigorous definition of this concept. I will merely make two observations. First, legalism involves the gradual expulsion of the concept of truth from the field of ethics; legalistic ethics are always, to a greater or lesser extent, bereft of truth. Indeed, the question of legalism is not "Which is good or evil?" (a question concerning the truth about good/evil), but "Is there a law pertaining to it?" (a question concerning obligation as such). My second observation is a consequence. In a legalistic context, the central question on the matter of conscience is this: "What is the connection between moral law and the recognition that one is under an obligation?" Let me explain. Since it is the law that imposes the obligation and since the individual is not placed under any obligation (by the law) unless he knows he is under an obligation, the central question is this: "What awareness of law places the individual under an obligation?" Formulated in these terms, the question had started down a theoretical road that would have led into a real maze.

Theoretical attention came to be focused increasingly on the subjective nature of the knowledge that the thinking subject has of the law: certain knowledge, doubtful knowledge, et cetera. The theme of true/false conscience was replaced by the concept of certain/doubtful conscience. The question, in other words, was this: In what conditions does the "recognition of being under an obligation" bind me? When is the judgment by which I recognize my obligation (= moral conscience) such that it really places me under an obligation (= takes away my freedom)? To grasp how profound this change was, even if it was a very subtle change, one observation will suffice. St. Thomas Aquinas would give the following reply to the above question: "per se, when the judgment is true; per accidens, even if–in certain conditions–it is false."[13]

Today, our reply is, "When it is a certain judgment." In short, attention has shifted from the truth of the judgment (of conscience) to the certitude with which the thinking subject consents. Truth is a property of judgment and implies the referral of the thinking subject to being. Certitude is a property of judgment and implies the referral of the thinking subject to his own judgment. Indeed, certitude signifies by and in itself a subjective state only, which has no reference to existence. I can be absolutely certain about something that is actually erroneous, and doubtful about something that is actually true. In this way the doctrine of conscience has gradually acquired an increasingly subjective inspiration. The doctrine of conscience has literally become the doctrine of the thinking subject, insofar as it forms itself or does not form itself under the obligation of the law.

Before we go any further, let us pause for a moment to consider the concept of autonomy (of conscience). In a classic vision autonomy means that only true judgment, that is, only an act of reason, can guide freedom. Only truth (a false judgment is not an act of reason) can give us the freedom that leads to beatitude. Autonomy of conscience, therefore, means: "Follow only truth; be rational in your choices; do not let yourself be guided by anything other than truth." And in actual fact, St. Thomas Aquinas's demonstration of the existence of moral law in his *Contra Gentes* (III, 114) is based wholly on this concept of autonomy. In the context of a doctrine of conscience centered on the problem of certitude, autonomy becomes a term with a different content. Autonomy now means the right of the thinking subject to construct his own certitude without anyone else being able to have a decisive say in the matter. We can now glimpse the insoluble difficulties that attend the problem of the relationship with the teaching authority of the church, as we will see more clearly later on. I would now like to resume our train of thought in order to reflect on the first change in meaning of the concept of autonomy.

The emphasis on the problem of certitude rather than on the problem of truth (of the judgment of conscience) led to the introduction into spiritual life of what we might call disorder in the relationship between the spiritual faculties. Let me explain. Despite all appearances to the contrary and despite the way in which the question has been handled, the problem of the relationship between will and reason is vitally important to human existence.[14] Put another way, once reflection ceases to be based predominantly on the relationship of the faculties to the subject and becomes a discourse on man, on the existing individual who, as a thinking subject, decides on his own eternal existence, it ceases to be a purely abstract construction. Now–and this has been noted by the finest interpreters of modernity–the leaning toward certitude is a voluntarist leaning. Assent in moral questions, which rarely rise to the level of incontrovertible evidence, is an act of will. Indeed, the whole of Christian teaching has always insisted on the need for "purity of the heart" in order to know the truth about good and evil. However, we now find ourselves in a different situation.

As the problem of truth is no longer central, it is no longer a question of an attitude or an openness to truth, where one is free from prejudice and simply has a disinterested desire to know. It is now a decision of conscience involving not truth itself but the certain opinion that something is true. The term and concept of judgment have been replaced by the concept of decision. "Wishing to highlight the 'creative' character of conscience, some authors no longer refer to its acts as 'judgments' but as 'decisions.' Only by making these decisions 'autonomously' may man attain his moral maturity."[15] Perhaps it is now easier to see what I meant when I talked about the introduction into spiritual life of a certain disorder in the relationship between one's faculties. Instead of keeping separate the planes of knowledge and will, the knowledge of truth has been emptied of its contents by the affirmation of the autonomy of the decision. I would like to show you the implications of this by drawing your attention to a number of theoretical facts.

The first fact. Freedom of conscience means consciousness of one's own freedom; indeed, the two are identical. In fact, freedom of conscience means that the judgment by which the thinking subject "tells" himself whether the act he is carrying out is right or wrong is a decision that has no external basis. For this reason, freedom belongs totally to conscience and conscience totally to freedom, in the sense that conscience (= the judgment that is conscience) does not refer ultimately to anything other than the decision of freedom. This is proven by the almost total disappearance of the theme of prudence and its judgment from ethical reflection. There was simply no longer any point in talking about it—conscience had taken its place.

The second fact. As it is now a question of "decisions" rather than "judgments," the true-false labels no longer have any real meaning. Conscience is always infallibly true. When it comes to decisions, there can no longer be any question of truth or falsehood. Indeed, B. Schüller writes: "Conscience cannot be mistaken when it comes to good and evil: that which it ordains is always and infallibly a moral good."[16] Instead of truth or falsehood, we should talk about authenticity and sincerity. We are each called upon to act according to our convictions, without having to ask ourselves about the truth or otherwise of these convictions. The individual simply places his trust in himself, in a sort of "self-basis" that seems the most perfect definition of despair, a truly mortal disease in contemporary man. True, some people still talk about the truth of conscience. However, they talk about this truth (of conscience) as if it were a truth of one's own character, with no universal value. Quite honestly, I cannot understand what all this can mean.[17]

The third fact. Radical "subjectivization," in other words, the total inclusion of conscience in free decision, has made it impossible to find any basis for civil law. This is because it has destroyed the very fabric of human sociality. The destruction of the social fabric is easily demonstrated. Human sociality is built both in and through the participation of each person's acts.[18]

Each act is obviously that of an individual. However, through the judgment of conscience, it takes root in the truth of the common good (in the Augustinian sense) of man as such. And in this sense, Vatican II sees in the loyalty to conscience an event of profound social communion.[19] If, as some have done, we deny that conscience is rooted in the truth of the common good, the affirmation of freedom becomes incompatible, as a principle, with the affirmation of any social construct that has not arisen from free negotiation—free negotiation that is founded on the basis of its own usefulness; neo-contractualism and utilitarianism meet up; justice is born out of agreement.

However, I would like to dwell chiefly on the problems facing the church. The newly constructed doctrine of conscience has introduced into Catholic doctrine the anti-ecclesiastical principle *per eminentiam*. This, I believe, explains many of the church's current problems. We can explain ourselves by first of all saying that the anti-ecclesiastical principle is the anti-Marian principle. And by "Marian principle" I mean obedient assent to revealed Truth, in which freedom is born and exalts itself to the utmost ("he who remains in me will bear much fruit"). The newly constructed doctrine of conscience leads to the affirmation of a rupture between the individual and the ecclesiastical mediation of revealed Truth, a cleavage between two great entities— that of individuality and that of the mediation of the church. Then comes the moment when the individual is alone, but in the sense of "self-basis," as I said earlier. Logically, the church can but recognize this decision, even if objectively it contradicts its own validity. I have referred to the uprooting of the individual from the church. This doctrine of conscience is not immediately anti-Petrine, but because it is anti-Marian it becomes anti-Petrine.

We can now bring to an end this first section, which I entitled "Diagnostic Reflection." To sum up briefly, the concept of autonomy that now predominates in the doctrine of moral conscience that actually generated this concept is the outcome of a secularist interpretation of Christian subjectivity—of an attempt, in other words, to draw up a doctrine of Christian subjectivity that disregards the fact that it generates this very subjectivity. The Catholic theology of conscience has sought to introduce this interpretation into Catholic doctrine. In reality, it has introduced a foreign body, which has ended up destroying that very same Catholic doctrine, as *Veritatis Splendor* teaches us.[20]

A Theoretical and Practical Proposition

I would like to begin my humble attempt to outline a positive proposition by returning to the concept of the "secularist interpretation" of Christian subjectivity with which I ended the first section. I would like to refer to a famous page in Hegel's *Geschichte der Philosophie*, in

which he maintains that only "in the Christian religion has the doctrine that says all men are equal before God made any headway because Christ attached them all to Christian freedom," but that when it
comes to "the concept, the knowledge that man is naturally free, this
science of the self is not an ancient one."[21] The meaning of this page is
clear: Only the principle of modernity has led us to examine Christianity fully in the light of its essential, anthropological core. Only the
principle of modernity has been able to give us a full and thorough
idea of subjective freedom, an exploit made possible only by the de-
tachment of dogmatic objectivity. Hegel's remarks only interest us
insofar as they show us that the confrontation between modernity and
Christianity has come about in the determination of this concept and
in the experience of freedom.

However, we cannot ignore the fact that the process of modernity
has already come to an end and has now been called into question
from within. This process has led to the emptying or deconstruction
of "modern subjectivity" and of the doctrine of moral conscience that
had fed on it, as I have already pointed out.

This end can therefore only be a beginning, in a radical sense: a
reconstruction of the human subjectivity and the freedom destroyed
by modernity and postmodernity on the philosophical side and, quite
often, on the theological side. Only within this reconstruction, or rather
foundation, can we find a true doctrine of moral conscience. In my
introduction I talked of a return to the home that had been aban-
doned in order to journey to a "faraway place." The son's first step is
to "re-enter himself" and regain his freedom, to become once more in
reality a thinking subject.

I would like to put forward a few simple, disjointed thoughts on
this sort of reconstruction. Let us begin by thinking about the experience of Moses. Let us imagine we are with him at perhaps the most
dramatic moment in his entire life. He finds himself trapped between
the Red Sea and Pharaoh's army. What is to be done? What possibilities are open to him? The first possibility would be to cross the sea on
foot. It is ridiculous even to contemplate such an idea, as it would
signify death. It is an impossible possibility. The second would be to
stand and fight Pharaoh. Absurd even to think of it–it would mean
going to meet certain death. It is an impossible possibility. The third
would be to retrace his footsteps, come to terms with Pharaoh and

return to slavery in Egypt. It is the only possible possibility. Yet by becoming part of Egypt once more, he would see his own identity and therefore his own freedom destroyed. He must choose between pure possibility, that is akin to pure fantasy and illusion, and pure necessity, in the shape of unchanged reality. So how does Moses escape this dilemma? By believing that everything is possible for God, even the parting of the waves to allow his people to cross the sea. By his act of faith, Moses becomes free and builds a new people, begins a new story. We never think enough about the abyss this act of faith represents. What does "to believe that everything is possible for God" mean? Well, it means to be certain of three things: that God can do everything, that God knows how to do everything, and that God wants to do everything for the one he loves. Man senses within himself the first stirrings of a project, of a story that is becoming possible: Moses leaves his entire existence in Egypt behind him. A feeling of necessity grows within man and he can no longer be other than thus: if necessary, God will even part the waves or bring the dead back to life. Human possibility is rooted in divine necessity, and human necessity is rooted in divine possibility.

How does this synthesis of necessity and possibility come about? Quite simply, this synthesis is called faithful obedience to one's own destiny, which also happens to be God's project. Without this synthesis, no proper existence can be constructed. An existence devoid of possibility is a lifeless existence, and an existence devoid of necessity is an empty existence. An existence devoid of possibility goes nowhere, and an existence devoid of necessity has nowhere to go.

This synthesis belongs at the balance point of the two poles. If we abandon this balance point, we do so at the expense of either necessity or possibility. In the first case, the person leaves his own reality and enters into the realm of sheer illusion. In the second case, the person never becomes himself. Kierkegaard says most perspicaciously that we need both vowels and consonants to be able to speak. The vowels represent possibility, the consonants necessity. A man devoid of possibility is dumb, as consonants on their own are incommunicable. A man devoid of necessity utters only meaningless sounds, as vowels on their own do not constitute meaning.[22] So when do we achieve this synthesis?

We now find ourselves at the core of human historicity, where human freedom and God's freedom meet. This meeting, I repeat, is called faithful obedience. We now understand how it is possible to come up with three different radical definitions of human historicity. Human history is the unfolding of a logical (i.e., real and rational) necessity, in which each event is but one sentence of an entire discourse. Human history is the accidental occurrence of insignificant possibilities. Human history is the history of the conjunction of divine and human freedom. In the case of the first definition, the greatness of the individual lies in his awareness of the historical process that is unfolding. In the case of the second definition, the greatness of the individual simply has no meaning. In the case of the third definition, the greatness of the individual consists of saintliness.

It is in this context, at the crossroads of divine and human freedom, that the judgment of conscience belongs. It is not the decision of freedom. The judgment of conscience comes before the decision of freedom and judges it. Any confusion between *iudicium conscientiae* and *iudicium electionis* leads inexorably to the emptying of Christian and human subjectivity.

Still less can we say that the judgment of conscience disregards God's freedom, which leads man to his ultimate destination in God's Wisdom. The judgment of conscience arises from the confrontation between an act that, in a given situation, presents itself as a possibility and the truth, goodness, and dignity of man, loved by God in Christ for all eternity. This truth, goodness, and dignity can be affirmed/denied, loved/hated, saved/lost precisely through man's acts.

It is in this context that we can understand what moral law is, what conscience is, and what the role of both is in the area of human and Christian subjectivity. Let us deal first with the nature of moral law. Once again, we will start with an example. Man has an inclination or instinct for sexual intercourse with a person of the opposite sex, and science has shown that sexuality is "designed" in such a way as to give birth to a new human being. Therefore, we can say that sexuality's own specific purpose—and I stress the word *specific*—is sexual union in order to create a new life. Can we say that it is also its due purpose (*debitus finis*) and that sexuality's specific purpose and sexuality's due purpose are one and the same thing? We must refute this identity, but why?

Rational man understands that: a) being somebody is essentially different and more than being something; b) the body is a personal body and the man is a corporeal person; c) sexuality, therefore, is personal sexuality and man is a sexual person ("man and woman he created them"). Man has gained knowledge of himself and, enlightened by the truth about himself, asks himself two questions. What exercise of sexuality and what sexual act will affirm this truth? What act will negate this truth? He arrives at the following conclusion: only an act of conjugal love open to the gift of life will affirm (i.e., realize) this truth. Any act other than this will negate (i.e., not realize) this truth. Once man has recognized this link between an act and the individual, he has discovered a moral law.

Therefore, in its essence, moral law literally means a judgment of reason that enables us to recognize the link between an act and an individual's existence, insofar as it is realizable (*perfectible*) through an act freely carried out. Moral law is this judgment.

By analogy, though, besides formally meaning the rational judgment that enables us to recognize the relationship between the act and the individual, moral law can also mean the very relationship itself. It is what we might call "wholesome food," in the sense of "food that brings good health." We can now see why "specific purpose" is not the same as "due purpose." Inclination as such is not moral law. Moral law constitutes itself through reason.

We must now look at the difference between the knowledge we attain through the rational judgment that is moral law and the knowledge we attain through the rational judgment that is moral conscience. The first type of knowledge is universal and only potentially particular; the second is particular and only potentially universal. Let me explain. When moral law considers the act of a specific individual, it looks neither at the circumstances in which this act can be carried out nor at the individual's intentions in carrying it out. Rather, it considers the act in and for itself, in its pure relationship with the individual as such, insofar as it can be the object of free will, and disregarding any other consideration contained in the desire to carry out this act.

It is easy to understand why this knowledge is universal; wherever we come across a human person carrying out this act, the affirmations of moral law will hold good. It is also easy to understand why this knowledge is potentially particular and therefore only remotely practicable. The act, such as it is considered by moral law, does not exist in the real world, in that the real act always has more to it than the act considered in this fashion. The knowledge is not false, but it is limited and incomplete.

This is why we need knowledge acquired through conscience. Conscience enables us to get to know the act in all its particularity. What we are talking about here is an act of practical reasoning, a judgment that enables man to find out the moral quality of the act he can carry out or is already carrying out. However, in order to understand properly the nature of this judgment and the knowledge it enables us to acquire, we must remember the distinction we made earlier between it and the judgment of choice. The judgment of conscience is a judgment that is per se purely rational. It says: "This is the action that I must/must not take in this situation." It is an appraisal of the action set in the context of its particular circumstances yet still considered on its own merits (i.e., independently of the individual's desires and intentions). This is why this type of judgment is not immediately practical, as ascertained by the fact that it can be contradicted by free choice. And, indeed, choice springs from man's will, desires, and intentions.

Even though it is a particular judgment, the judgment of conscience also requires a degree of universality. That is, it has a justification of its own that is not based on references so personal as to be inexpressible and incommunicable. In the judgment of conscience, the individual says at the same time: "This is the action I must take" *and* "Anyone in my position should take this action." From where does conscience derive this capacity to be both a particular and a universal judgment? We will now turn to another important dimension of the judgment of conscience.

Reason formulates its own judgments according to universal and necessary laws. Conscience is a rational judgment, whose subject is an act looked at in the context of the greatest possible number of circumstances but judged in the light of the individual's truth and dignity. When my conscience says, "This is the action I must take," it does so because it has seen that in this action the human being as such will be affirmed and fulfilled. I have deliberately said "the human being," rather than "myself," as conscience does not pass judgment according to that which pleases me or is useful to me, that which "*tamquam privato sui ipsius amore desiderat anima*,"[23] following on from St. Augustine (*Sermo* 8,9). It is in this that the greatness (but also the paucity) of conscience resides. Through it, man becomes aware of his truth as an individual, of the goodness inherent to his own personal being and of his singular preciousness as an individual, but only insofar as this truth demands here and now to be affirmed, not denied, this goodness demands here and now to be loved, not hated, and this preciousness demands here and now to be saved, not lost. As conscience sees the act as a means of bringing about this affirmation, love, and salvation, the act is deemed to be right and proper. It is because of his conscience that man becomes "imprisoned" within his own truth, in that he is now constrained to be free and to make his own choices. In this sense, conscience sets man free. It sets him free because it subjects him to truth. It is because we are subjected to truth, writes St. Augustine, that we are free.[24] It is precisely this profound relationship among conscience, truth, and choice that enables us to explain in which sense we can and must talk about the autonomy of conscience.

The first sense, from which I believe all the others flow, is that man cannot make a free choice without the mediation of the judgment of his conscience. He can only make a free choice insofar as he follows the judgment of his conscience and because of the fact that *is* the judgment of his conscience. In this sense, then, man must always follow the judgment of his conscience, because quite simply he must act humanly, that is to say, freely. To act according to one's conscience and to act freely are like the condition and the conditioned.

Consequently, autonomy of conscience means that man must not let himself be guided in his appraisal by his passions and desires, but solely by his pure and disinterested desire to know the truth about the choice and the act that will affirm his personal existence. He must not be swayed by considerations of usefulness or calculations of any sort. As soon as he begins to look out of the corner of his eye at the useful or damaging consequences of his act, he says goodbye to autonomy of conscience.

Autonomy of conscience means not accepting the criterion of the greater number as a criterion of truth about what is good or evil and not following the opinion of the majority. *Familiaris Consortio* puts it marvelously: "By following Christ, the church seeks truth, which is not always the same thing as the opinion of the majority. It listens to conscience, not power, and thereby defends the poor."[25] Autonomy of conscience means the ability to arrive at a judgment free from the conditioning of popular opinion and free from one's own passions and interests, solely in one's submission to truth.

Given the nature of moral law, the specificity of the judgment of conscience, and the relationship between the two, we are now at a stage where we can ask ourselves about the role conscience plays in human and Christian subjectivity. This is a very important point. Let us go back to an example I mentioned earlier. It is clear that man feels a natural inclination, preceding his will, to have intercourse with a person of the opposite sex. Yet it is equally certain that this intercourse will only humanly come about if it can be done freely. Freedom is called upon to assume this inclination, since that toward which it inclines is a human good.

However, this is precisely the point: what does it incline toward exactly? Or, put another way, what specific good comes of sexuality? What does the goodness of sexuality really consist of? This is a rational question. In other words, reason must come up with an answer. In what sense must it? In the sense that man must explain this inclination to himself and within himself. In the sense that it is up to reason to come up with a picture of goodness that freedom will then use to move man to make his choices. Now, reason can find the good that is both possible (*operabile*) and due (*operandum*). "Due good" belongs to the rational will, and the latter must choose it if it does not want to repudiate and destroy itself at the very moment it affirms itself. We now have the answer to the question we asked earlier: the role of the moral law in human subjectivity is to bring to light each man's due good. "Due" means the original suitability in which good (indicated by moral law) and rational will belong to each other. This good is the person's own specific good, to which the rational will is oriented.

Moral law and conscience represent the two fundamental moments in which spiritual life is realized in the quest for truth about individual good. They are two stages along the same path toward the knowledge of the truth about what is good. They are rooted in the spiritual attitude that the Ancients called *synderesis*, that is, the innate capacity of the intellect to apprehend goodness and generate within itself the notion of good and the supreme principles of moral order. And they are rooted in man's spiritual reach toward the plenitude of existence, which moves him to search for a means of attaining freedom, that is, to search for the truth about what is good. It is to this purpose, which is shared by conscience and by moral law, that I would like to draw your attention.

If, assisted by descriptions of all the great masters from Plato to Newman, we become sufficiently aware of the spiritual event that is ethical experience, we will see that the latter is the experience of a goodness that demands to be recognized and loved by us–not because we are us, rather than other people, but because we are rational subjects. It is the rational will as such that is called into question; therefore, every rational will is called into question, whether that of God or that of a creature, angel or man. Ethical experience is the perception of an order that is intrinsic to existence as such, a measure that transcends every existence and is immanent to every existence.

However, ethical experience is not only this. It calls on our uniqueness, which means nobody can take the place of another. It is through a choice of my very own making that I am asked to recognize and love the good and the order that are intrinsic to existence. Ethical experience is this conjunction of universality and singularity, of eternity and temporality. It is the breath of eternity in time. This is why the knowledge of good comes to us through a vision (= moral law) of an order that must take shape in our very concrete choice and through a vision (= moral conscience) of the specific good of this concrete choice in the light of the order of existence. It is like a circle that initiates itself in the life of the spirit.

When does this "circle" break up? When we set conscience and moral law against each other? It is precisely this internal disarticulation that has taken place over recent years. The break in the relationship occurs when the concept of truth is expelled from ethical reflection. This expulsion means that the human heart's demand for happiness can no longer receive a response that can be qualified as either true or false. Asking oneself whether it is possible to distinguish between true and false happiness no longer has any meaning, since to be happy means to *feel* happy. Accordingly, the project of one's individual existence eludes every judgment that has a degree of universal validity. The same thing applies to the choices that bring about the fulfillment of that project.

Conclusion

The judgment of conscience is the last tangential point of divine Wisdom bestowed on man along with free decision. Saving man's true autonomy from either the desubjectivization of postmodernity or what we called earlier "self-basis" is one of the fundamental tasks of current Christian thinking. In order to save the truth of freedom.

Notes

1. See, for example, S. Pinckaers, *Les sources de la moral chrètienne* (Fribourg-Paris: University Press Fribourg, 1985), pp. 258-279; *The Sources of Christian Ethics*, trans. Mary T. Noble (Washington, D.C.: Catholic University of America Press, 1995).

2. PG 13, 45 A.

3. PG 13, 45 A.

4. Lib. III; *Die Griechischen Christi.* Scriftsteller, vol. 33, Leipzig 1925, p. 190, 19-20;
p. 191, 18-19.

5. See, for example, F. Dreyfus, "L'actualisation à l'intérieur de la Bible," *Revue Biblique* 33 (1976), p. 161.

6. LXVIII, 1. *S. Bernardi opera*, vol. 2 (Rome: Ed. Cistercienses, 1958), p. 196.

7. *S. Bernardi opera*, vol. 1 (Rome: Ed. Cistercienses, 1958), p. 67.

8. 10 July 1993. See the text in *Herder Korrespondenz* (September 1993), pp. 460-467, especially IV, 4, p. 465.

9. See, for example, P. P. Ottonello, *Struttura e forma del nichilismo europeo*, 4 vol. (Rome, 1990-92); G. Perrati, *Contemporaneità e post-moderno* (Milan, 1992); A. Touraine, *Critica della modernità* (Milan, 1993).

10. See A. Polaino-Lorente, *Manual de bioetica general*, Introduction, pp. 23-30.

11. A. Manzoni, "Del sistem che fonda la morale sull'utilità," in *Osservazioni sulla morale cattolica*, vol. 2 (Milane-Naples, 1966), pp. 325-410.

12. Cf. studies by S. Pinckaers in particular (see note 1).

13. Cf. Aquinas, *Summa Theologiae*, IaIIae, q.19, a.5 and a.6.

14. Cf. C. Fabro, "La dialettica d'intelligenza e volontà nella constituzione dell'atto livero," in *Doctor Communis* 2 (1977), pp. 163-191.

15. *Veritatis Splendor*, 55, 2.

16. B. Schüller, *La Fondazione Eei Guidizi Morali* (Assisi, 1975), p. 75.

17. Cf. *Veritatis Splendor* 56, 1.

18. K. Wojtyla, *Persona e atto* (Città del Vaticano, 1982), p. 287.

19. *Gaudium et Spes* 16: "*Fidelitate erga conscientiam christiani cum ceteris hominibus coniunguntur ad veritatem inquirendam et tot problemata moralia, quae tam in vita singulorum quam in sociali consortione exurgunt, in veritate solvenda.*"

20. Cf., for example, nos. 4,2; 29,4; 32,2.

21. G. F. Hegel, *Geschichte der Philosophie*, vol. 1, ed. Michelet (Berlin, 1840), p. 63; also cf. *Grundlinien der Philosophie des Rechts*, Vorrede, ed. Hoffmeister (Hamburg, 1955), p. 17.

22. The most profound of Kierkegaard's insights into freedom is in *La malattia mortale*. About possibility-necessity see *Parte Prima*, C, A, b, in *Opere* (Florence, 1972), pp. 637-641.

23. *S. Bernardi Opera*, vol. 6 (Rome: Ed. Cistercienses, 1958), p. 37.

24. In *De Libero Arbitrio* II, XIII, 37; CC 29, p. 262.

25. *Familiaris Consortio*, 5, 2.

Index

Abelard, 20n.19
abortion, 22, 25, 46
absolution, 138
accountability, 117-18
adultery, 123
Alfonso, St., 149
anamnesis, 12-15, 16, 88
Anthony, St., 87
anthropology, 34-35
anti-Marian principle, 158
Aquinas, St. Thomas
  on autonomy, 155
  on Christ's passion, 45
  Christian morality in, 80
  on conditioned necessity, 98
  and conflicts of conscience, 140
  on *conscientia*, 15-16
  on deliberation, 101-2
  distinction between conscience and
    prudence in, 89-91
  on the divine image, 57
  on first principles, 96
  on freedom, 65, 82
  on free will, 62
  and God's presence, 56
  on the goodness of creation, 40
  on growth of charity, 91-92
  on human nature, 39
  importance of conscience in, 149
  on the *liberum arbitrium*, 58
  moral law in, 70
  on the *ordo amoris*, 124, 132
  on *perplexitas*, 99-100
  on prudence, 87

Quaestio Disputata de Veritate, 102-3
  on *synderesis*, 87-88
  virtue-based morality of, 86
  on the will, 61-62
Aristotle, 94, 96
atheism, 41
Augustine, St., 9, 13, 14, 19n.18, 46-
  47, 164
authority and freedom, 1-2, 8
autonomy, 27-28, 33, 38, 41, 155-56

Balthasar, Hans Urs von, 17
Basil, St., 12-13, 14, 83
Belmans, I. G., 19n.19
Belmens, Theo, 100, 101, 103-4,
  109n.27
Bernard, St., 150-51
Beyond Freedom and Dignity, 30
Blessed Mother, 47

Caffarra, Carlo, 44-45
Calvin, John, 31
Carrasco, Ignacio, 43
Catechism of the Catholic Church, 84, 86,
  144
certitude, 6-7, 155
charity
  blocking of, 72
  growth of, 91-92
  manifestation of, 56
  morality of, 83
  and prudence, 86
  and the transformation of the will,
    66

169

Chiavacci, Enrico, 144-45
Christian ethics, 116, 118, 130
Christian memory, 15, 18
church, 150-52, 137-38
communism, 52
connatural knowledge, 91-92
conscience
  and authority, 2, 8
  autonomy of, 164-65
  binding of, 94, 98-101
  conflicts of, 138, 139-40, 142-44
  creativity of, 52, 74, 135, 145
  definitions of, 4, 6-7, 21, 36-37
  destruction of, 152-53
  erroneous, 4-5, 16, 90, 94-95, 99-101
  infallibility of, 2, 18n.1, 157
  judgment of, 127-28, 161, 163-64
  justifying power of, 4-5
  loss of, 21-22
  medieval doctrine of, 12
  primacy of, 8
  rational structure of, 60
  shift in importance of, 149-50
conscientia, 15-16
conscientious objection, 128-29
consequentialism, 121-22, 123, 124, 130
consilium, 101-2
contraception, 125, 129, 142
convictions, 157
creation, doctrine of, 38-39, 40
creativeness, 64-65
Crossing the Threshold of Hope, 27
cultural coordinates, 24
culture
  crisis of, 24, 25-26
  desensitizing of, 25
  effects of, 24
  papal concern for, 25
  restoration of, 45

Decalogue. *See* Ten Commandments
decisions, 156
deliberation, 101-2

deontological ethics, 121, 122
Dignitatis Humanae, 40, 100
Dionysius the Areopagite, 123
disagreement, 95-97
divine guidance, 70
divorce, 129, 151
Dominum et Vivificantem, 22
due good, 165

Eastern Europe, 6-7
ecclesiastical law, 139
education, 59-60
emotions
  guidance of, 69
  repression of, 67, 68-69, 71
ethical experience, 166
ethics
  deontological, 121, 122
  effect of circumstances on, 122-23
  of responsibility, 111-12, 119-20
  teleological, 121-22, 123, 124, 130
  see also Christian ethics
euthanasia, 22, 46, 130-31
Evangelium Vitae, 21, 25-26, 46
existentialism, 39

faith, 3, 36, 160
faithful obedience, 160, 161
Familiaris Consortio, 164-65
Fichte, Johann Gottlieb, 18n.1, 131
first principles, 95-97
Fletcher, Joseph, 37
free choice, 65-66
freedom
  and authority, 1-2, 8
  binding of, 153
  church's perspective on, 51
  of conscience, 156-57
  definition of, 53, 58, 82
  for excellence, 81-82
  of indifference, 80-81
  main function of, 52
  and moral choices, 52
  subjective, 159
  true, 43

and truth, 164
in *Veritatis Splendor*, 29-30, 41, 42
free will, 62, 98, 102
Freud, Sigmund, 69
fundamental option, 29, 41

Gaudium et Spes, 84, 100, 143-44
God
  necessity of, 37, 42-43, 131
  presence of, 56
Goffi, Tullo, 138
Görres, Albert, 5
gospel, 117
grace, 17-18, 62
guilt, 60
guilt feelings, 5
Gutiérrez, Gustavo, 33

happiness, 166
Häring, Bernard, 138
Hegel, Georg Wilhelm Friedrich, 158-59
heteronomy, 27-28, 41
Hitler, Adolf, 5, 16
Holy Spirit, 67, 73
human nature, 39-40
human sociality, 157

ideology, 71
ignorance, 99-100
image of God, 11-12, 57
Institutioni Juris Ecclesiasticii, 129
Instructions on liberation theology, 33-34
intellectual repression, 71-72
iudicium, 109n.27

James, William, 38
Jerome, St., 88
John Paul II, 21, 22, 25, 34-35, 44
judgment, 16, 63

Kant, Immanuel, 27-29, 117
Kierkegaard, Søren, 160
knowledge, 98-99, 115, 153-55, 162-63

Königsteiner Erklärung, 129

law. *See* moral law
legalism, 154
liberation theology, 33-34
liberty. *See* freedom
liberum arbitrium
  role of reason in, 58
  role of will in, 58
  significance of, for Aquinas, 57
Logos, 11, 18
love
  for God, 83
  as motivator, 118
  spark of, 13
Lowell, James Russell, 26
Luther, Martin, 30, 31, 124

MacIntyre, Alasdair, 107n.7
Magisterium, 2, 145
manual tradition, 79-80, 81
marriage vows, 123
martyrs, 131
Marxism, 32-34, 131
McInerny, Ralph, 43
meaning, 39
military service, 128-29
mission, 13-14
modernity, 159
moral choice, 52-53
moral education, 69-70, 74
morality, 1-2, 42
moral law
  effect of pastoral solutions on, 145
  function of, 60
  and heteronomy, 41
  in Kant, 28
  and moral theology, 54
  nature of, 161-62
  necessity of, 83-84
  reception of, 70
  source of, 84
  See also natural moral law
moral obligation, 153-54
moral systems, 139-40

moral theology
  based on the Ten Commandments,
    79-80
  definition of, 54-55
  and God's presence, 56, 73
  organizing center of, 54
  and spiritual repression, 72
  as theology, 55-56
  virtue-based, 80, 85
More, Thomas, 9, 22-23
murder, 129

natural moral law, 96-97, 127, 130
  See also moral law; *synderesis*
Nazism, 32, 122
necessity, 98, 160
Neuhaus, Richard John, 51
neurotic personality, 60
Newman, John Henry
  *On Consulting the Faithful in Matters
    of Doctrine*, 104-5
  A Letter to the Duke of Norfolk, 105
  on the papacy, 8, 105
  place of conscience in, 8-10, 21, 84
  on religion and morality, 43
  toast of, 8, 14, 105
norms, 124-25

obedience, 70-71
ordo amoris, 124, 132
Orestes, 17
Origen, 150
original sin, 65-66
Ottaviani, Alfredo, 129

pacifism, 119
papacy
  power of, 15
  relationship to conscience, 8, 105-
    6
  true nature of, 14
passion of Christ, 45-46
pastoral solutions
  defense for, 143-45
  defined, 136-38

elements of, 141-42
erroneous solutions of, 139
moral significance of, 145-46
in *Veritatis Splendor*, 135
perplexitas, 99
personal encounter, 71-72
Pieper, Josef, 38, 39
Planned Parenthood vs. Casey, 37-38
possibility and necessity, 160
postmodernity, 152
power, 11
practical atheism, 36, 37
practical reason, 59, 63-64
practical reasoning, 94, 107n.2
predestination, 31
presuppositions, 24, 26
primordial knowledge, 13-14
principia reflexa, 140
private interpretation, 31
probabilism, 81
progress, 10
promises, 123
Protestantism, 30-32
prudence, 86-87, 88-92, 157
psychopathic personality, 60

Quaestio Disputata de Veritate, 102-3

Rahner, Karl, 100-101, 132
rationalization, 71
Ratzinger, Joseph, 88, 97
reason, 30, 47, 58, 59, 63-64
relativism, 10, 29, 37-38
relativity theory, 10
religion, 36
repressive process, 68-69
responsibility
  and accountability, 117-18
  for consequences, 119-25, 126-27
  and conviction, 111-12
  criteria for, 127
  effect of complexity on, 114
  grading, 124
  and inactivity, 115-16
  and knowledge, 115

limits of, 112-13
and love, 118
moral, 117
for oneself, 131-33
political, 113-14, 126
and social sub-systems, 114-15
spheres of, 113-14

salus animarum, 136, 137
salvation, 137, 146
salvation through ignorance, 3-7
Sartre, Jean-Paul, 39, 132
Schockenhoff, E., 18n.1
Schüller, B., 157
self-righteousness, 5-6
sensus fidelium, 104
sex, 68-69, 104, 161-62, 165
Situation Ethics, 37
Skinner, B. F., 30
social conformity, 4
Socrates, 11
sola Scriptura, 31
Spaemann, Robert, 40-41
speculative reason, 63
spiritual repression, 72
Stalin, Joseph, 5, 16
state, 128-29
subjectivism, 9, 29, 31, 94-95
subjectivization, 157
submission, 148
synderesis
  judgments of, 97
  meaning of, 12, 87-89, 165
  and practical reason, 59
  See also anamnesis; natural moral
    law

teleological ethics, 120-22, 123, 124,
  130
Ten Commandments, 42, 83

theological ethics, 55
theology, 55
theoretical reason, 59
total depravity, 30-31
totalitarianism, 32-35
truth
  arduousness of, 17-18
  attraction toward, 59
  and certitude, 155
  and infallible conscience, 2, 157
  necessity of, 38, 147-48
  in Newman, 8-9
  and relativity, 10-11

United Nations Conference on Development and Population, 44
utilitarian democracies, 35
utilitarianism, 121-22, 123, 124, 130

Veritatis Splendor
  on confusion between good and
    evil, 21
  on the Decalogue, 83
  on dissent, 26
  on freedom, 29-30, 53, 81-82
  on hope, 45
  on moral theology, 54-55
  on objective reality, 37, 38
  on pastoral solutions, 135
  on self-interest, 41-42
virtue-based morality, 85-86
virtue, 85, 86
voluntarism, 82, 146

Weber, Max, 111, 119
Westminster Confession of Faith, 31
will
  and *liberum arbitrium*, 58
  nature of, 61-62
  transformation of, 66-67